DRY ROT

IN THE IVORY TOWER

*A Case for Fumigation,
Ventilation, and Renewal
of the Academic Sanctuary*

John R. Campbell

University Press of America,® Inc.
Lanham • New York • Oxford

Copyright © 2000 by
University Press of America, ® Inc.
4720 Boston Way
Lanham, Maryland 20706

12 Hid's Copse Rd.
Cumnor Hill, Oxford OX2 9JJ

Library of Congress Cataloging-in-Publication Data

Campbell, John R.
Dry rot in the ivory tower: a case for fumigation, ventilation,
and renewal of the academic sanctuary / John R. Campbell
p.cm.
Includes bibliographical references and index.
1.   Education, Higher—Aims and objectives—United States. 2.
Universities and colleges—United States—Sociological aspects. I. Title.
LA227.4.C36   2000   378.73—dc21   99—462211 CIP

ISBN 0-7618-1646-1 (pbk: alk. ppr.)

CONTENTS

FOREWORD

Judith E. N. Albino, Ph.D., President
California School of Professional Psychology
President Emerita, University of Colorado

In 1946, an enormous incoming freshman class at Harvard, swelled by a huge influx of veterans, heard then-president James B. Conant assert that a college education should be for the sole purpose of improving the nation and the society. To do it well, he said, would require technical competence in science and engineering, political skills in government, a human perception of the goals of society, and a personal knowledge of the ends of life that could come only from the humanities. We should, he concluded, get on with this task of learning, jointly, not separately.[1]

What an eloquent synopsis of the mission of higher education!

Five decades later, in a book titled *The Uses of the University*, Clark Kerr, former president of the University of California, warned that universities were in danger of becoming "separate academic disciplines and departments held together by a central heating system and common disputes over parking," where important decisions would be based on "a division of the spoils rather than a determination of the goals".[2]

Could a fractious institution like the one described by Clark Kerr carry out the collective mission advanced by James Conant? I don't think so, and neither does this book's author, John Campbell. *Dry Rot in the Ivory Tower* is a heartfelt and angry call to arms, asking us all to look squarely at what we have either wrought, or allowed to flourish, in higher education.

I have long held the view that the mission of higher education is akin to a religious calling. It demands a vigilant commitment to a set of core values and a total dedication to the life of the mind. And, rather like religion, which often expects its ministers to forego material rewards in order to focus selflessly on higher ideals, higher education asks something similar of those of us who center our professional lives on the generation, communication, and application of knowledge for the benefit of our students and of society as a whole.

As a child growing up in West Tennessee, "going to college" was my greatest dream. I was profoundly grateful when the opportunity came, and I took full advantage to study, to broaden my horizons, to be challenged, and to develop myself intellectually, personally, and professionally. So entranced was I with this world of learning that I pursued at least six majors and attended four institutions before finally receiving my baccalaureate degree at the University of Texas in Austin. I often say that I never heard of a topic that I didn't want to study, and I never saw a college or university that I didn't want to attend. The halls of academe have been, for me, a truly sacred place, and I was struck, as a young woman, by an unmistakable call to dedicate myself to serving people and society as a scholar and a teacher, a passion that endures today.

I was fortunate to receive encouragement from family and respected mentors and role models. Later, I came to appreciate that the history of higher education in the United States had been shaped by many accomplished, and always idealistic, people – individuals such as Edward Everett, the former Massachusetts governor and president of Harvard, who said, "Education is a better safeguard of liberty than a standing army." I always have believed him, and I still do.

As a nation of people in a relatively young country, the residents of the United States of America can be legitimately proud of our system of higher education, surely one of our most estimable collective achievements. Ours is often acknowledged as the best educational system in the world. That is obvious not only in the achievements of our scientists and scholars, but also in the diversity of our institutions and offerings. In the United States, virtually anyone – with appropriate effort, but regardless of the quality of or deficits in preparation and ability – can be admitted and succeed in postsecondary education. There is literally a place for everyone: from trade and technical schools and community colleges to highly selective private institutions, as well as state colleges and universities and specialized institutions of every type imaginable. Consequently, countless men and women have grasped better lives for themselves and their children through the pursuit and attainment of higher education. I am immensely proud of, and support, any effort to preserve and protect this rich and precious legacy.

John Campbell's book is just such an effort. *Dry Rot in the Ivory Tower* could only have been written by someone who cares deeply about higher education, and felt himself compelled to call attention to the gradual but pernicious proliferation of inappropriate and even destructive forces operating at college campuses across the nation every day, threatening our institutional legitimacy as well as the public's confidence in our ability to carry out the mission of educating a new generation of social contributors.

As Clark Kerr predicted, governance on many college campuses has become driven by the wrong considerations. Politics have become so large a part of academic life that the motives for decisions often have little to do with the best interests of the most important university constituency: its students. In too many places, faculty have become accustomed to decision-making that is based on political expediency rather than the merits of ideas. Consequently, even when mission-driven leadership does emerge, the best intentions are often disbelieved. In such a climate, even the most selfless and dedicated leaders may be mistrusted.

This state of affairs is particularly distressing because faculty have historically been the most important line of defense against corruption, the most vigilant safeguarders of the educational mission. In my early faculty years, I was surrounded by just such scholars and academic administrators at the University at Buffalo (State University of New York) and collaborating colleagues at other major research universities across the country. These were people dedicated to the community of scholars; they encouraged and inspired me, and collectively we nourished our students and advanced the search for truth. But in more recent years, I have seen something else – faculty engaged in vicious competition with one another in what is perceived as a zero-sum game; other faculty pandering to administrators who are all too willing to pay them off in the name of avoiding conflict and political controversy.

What has happened, I wonder, to our commitment to the life of the mind? To our higher calling?

When John Campbell asked me to read his manuscript, I was at first taken aback by the title. The term "dry rot" particularly offended me. But I am not a biological scientist so I consulted expert sources and learned a little about what "dry rot" really is. Dry rot is caused by the growth of fungus in wood. Like other living organisms, it requires a food source, oxygen, and favorable temperature – i.e., sustenance and an environment in which it can flourish. It is also easy to acquire, but hard to get rid of. According to Webster, fungi "must live as saprophytes or parasites".

As some of the more appalling vignettes in John Campbell's book demonstrate, poor and even counter-productive leadership in the ivory tower is similarly easy to "acquire," and hard to eradicate. Like dry rot or any other parasitic organism, it has every reason to hold fast to its source of sustenance, little reason to let go. But as the book further demonstrates: even those of us charged with spotting, identifying, and rooting out such infestations have, in some cases, become part of the problem. The very structure of our bureaucracies may be rewarding a *laissez-faire* posture on the part of our most senior leaders.

I am distressed by the situations that have given rise to John Campbell's cautionary book. Indeed, the very title conjures up images of violation, infection, blight, corruption, and ruin. The metaphor is upsetting, but unfortunately, as the book demonstrates, in some cases all too apt.

My own experience has been that, in a variety of positions and places within the academy, and with increasing frequency, fewer and fewer leaders in higher education exhibit the value-laden zeal that would inoculate our institutions of higher education against the critical problems facing academia today. They are too eager to protect their positions by appeasing the political constituencies that can, in fact, undo them. And those who do speak up for the truth are often stymied, their leadership role having been seriously eroded by faculties holding an increasingly diverse set of values, people for whom "academic freedom" – a notion that I cherish – is interpreted to mean "every faculty member is his or her own boss". A powerful new wave of situational ethics has moved in. For many, a frenetic, selfish pursuit of power and personal gain has replaced the great ideals of the academy as the basic motivator.

Former British Prime Minister Margaret Thatcher has quoted Lord Acton when he said, "All power tends to corrupt, and absolute power corrupts absolutely." Few people know that, prior to her illustrious work in government, Lady Thatcher enjoyed an earlier career as a research chemist, having earned her Master's degree at Oxford University. Could it be that she first gained her insight into the corrupting nature of absolute power not in the halls of Parliament, but in a university setting?

Dr. Campbell's vignettes detail real occurrences. His stories tell of professors who shortchange students, and academic leaders who simply are not up to the admittedly difficult and complex job of maintaining standards while remaining accountable to disparate and demanding constituencies.

The book's account of the actions of powerful but self-interested university governing board members echoes the findings of a 1996 Commission on the Academic Presidency, sponsored by the Association of Governing Boards of

Universities and Colleges. Chaired by former Virginia Governor Gerald L. Baliles, the commission's report states:

> Unfortunately, too many trustees lack a basic understanding of higher education or a significant commitment to it. In extensive interviewing, the commission found instance after instance in which boards were either inadequately engaged with their institutions or, conversely, inappropriately involved in detail ... . Whether on public or private boards, what this adds up to is a significant problem: Many trustees understand neither the concept of service on a board as a public trust nor their responsibilities to the entire institution ... . A president saddled with a board incapable of exercising its trust responsibly and well is a badly weakened leader.[3]

The report further emphasizes that the problem is especially insidious at public institutions, where board members are often appointed – or worst of all, elected – in the context of partisan politics.

What John Campbell's book does so well is to illustrate what all this really means in everyday human terms – in the nature of the specific interactions between university constituents: students, faculty, administrators, executives, board members, and politicians. He renders, in his carefully chosen and representative vignettes, many of the ways in which our students and our institutions lose out under current circumstances.

Another area where we are remiss – one that I have spent a lot of time talking and writing about – is university athletics.

Having served as president of a National Collegiate Athletics Association Division 1A institution and as a former member and chair of the Presidents Commission of the NCAA, I have become extremely concerned with how our colleges and universities participate in what I have called a "conspiracy against youth" – particularly those from inner cities and disadvantaged communities.

Of course, every college or university president worthy of the office has learned to say that our athletes are admitted just like any other students; that our athletics programs are learning experiences that build character and skills; that those experiences are equally available to female as well as male students of all races; and that we never put dollars into athletic programs that could support academic activities.

But these claims, while they may be attainable goals, are simply untrue at this juncture. The dishonesty endangers people. It hurts the super-athletes who move on from college without a degree or without an education. And it contributes to a milieu in which many young people adopt inappropriate and impossible dreams of athletic stardom that undermine the time-proven value of education as the safest and most effective route to a fulfilling life and long-term personal success. Athletics should enhance the educational experience, not supplant it.

I believe that as long as we fail to face the truth about the management of intercollegiate athletics, we will continue to deal with excesses and corruption in our institutions, and young people who could experience the advantages of full participation in higher education will instead experience exploitation of their talents.

And, like John Campbell, I passionately want to see the plethora of ethical issues in higher education addressed. I have said that reform efforts in intercollegiate athletics must have their impetus in a single principle: that student athletes must be students first, and that their educations must come first. I'll now broaden that assertion to say that the whole spectrum of unethical activities surfacing at our colleges and universities – a spectrum so vividly revealed in this book's vignettes – will only be combated through the reinstatement of stewardship based on core values, so that the people in charge find their way by using a moral compass that points perpetually towards the basic mission of higher education.

To lean on Dr. Campbell's metaphor one more time: dry rot exists to thrive, grow, and perpetuate itself. By contrast, wood, once it's off the tree, is rather dormant and vulnerable. It must be actively protected from the elements that combine to allow infestation. It must be cared for by people for whom its structural integrity is of paramount importance.

For universities, John Campbell is one of those people. In *Dry Rot in the Ivory Tower*, he draws upon experiences and observations from four decades as a distinguished faculty member and college- and university-level administrator. This book came about because he felt compelled to come clean and blow the whistle, to sound a wake-up call, and to articulate his own particular array of feelings and notions about the fundamental problems responsible for the current state of affairs in higher education, and to then offer suggestions for extricating ourselves from these terrible dilemmas. All who care about the future of our country and our world should be grateful to him for that alone. That his diagnoses are so salient and his remedial prescriptions so straightforward constitute a wonderful bonus!

Along with this book's author, I am optimistic that the critical problems of our higher education system can be resolved and put right. This optimism is justified, I believe, because it must be and will be the public who will ultimately respond. Thomas Jefferson made it clear: "Whenever things get so far wrong as to attract their notice, the people, if well-informed, may be relied upon to set them right." John Campbell has taken it upon himself to serve up a clear and disturbing picture of how it is in many of today's colleges and universities. Now the ball is in the people's court.

J.E.N.A.

---

[1]As cited in "Ethics and the Proper Function of a University," Hosmer, LaRue Tone, paper presented at the Conference on Values in Higher Education at the University of Tennessee, Knoxville, TN, April 1996
[2]*The Uses of the University*, Kerr, Clark, Harvard University Press, Boston, 1995 (as cited in Hosmer, loc. cit.)
[3]*Renewing the Academic Presidency: Stronger Leadership for Tougher Times*, Association of Governing Boards of Universities and Colleges, Washington, DC, 1996

Acknowledgments

Any author incurs obligations during a major writing project. My indebtedness is unusually great. Students, staff, and professional colleagues (fellow faculty members and academic administrators) at numerous colleges and universities throughout the United States have shared experiences and philosophies that served as the bases for the themes and vignettes I have compiled, organized, and now divulge in this book. The collective concern of these people about the current state of affairs of higher education and their continuing encouragement for me to verbalize the problems were potent motivators in my decision to write the book.

From the start of this project, I have enjoyed the support of and wise feedback from my spouse Eunice and daughters Kathy and Karen. My long-term professional colleague, Dr. Stanley E. Curtis, shares with me a deep appreciation for the benefits of higher education to individuals and nations as well as a serious concern about the direction of higher education in the United States today. It has been my good fortune to be able to count on Dr. Curtis for his special kind of editorial assistance from the time this book was being conceptualized.

Great appreciation also is expressed to Benita Bale for her efficient clerical assistance and editorial suggestions.

I hope readers and, ultimately, our cherished and essential higher education system will benefit from the final product.

John R. Campbell
President Emeritus
Oklahoma State University
April 2000

THE TALES OF TWO STUDENTS

Chance favors the prepared mind.
Louis Pasteur (1822-1895)
French biologist and chemist

Tim Ballew was the second in a family of seven children. He would be the only one of them to attend and graduate from college. Today Tim Ballew presides over an international food-service chain that enjoys immense success. He also chairs a private foundation chartered to support underprivileged students as they pursue their educational goals.

Tim Ballew's life has followed the script of one version of the American dream. It began with the two older boys sleeping on a fold-up cot in the kitchen of a tarpaper shack in shantytown, "on the other side of the tracks". His second-generation-immigrant parents laid the foundation by instilling in him fundamental morals and values, including a strong work ethic. Those character traits have served him well in his 30-year rise from indigent poverty to global corporate leadership.

The elder Ballews believed in the American dream. They believed that one's contributions to society and other successes derive from ambition, attitude, education, and hard work. They admonished their children to always exceed the expectations of the employer. And that Tim did, as a paper-route entrepreneur, yard-worker, and shoe-shiner while in middle school; car-washer and grocery carry-out boy in high school; and student employee and pizza deliverer attending college.

A top scholar in his high school class, Tim Ballew was encouraged by several teachers to attend nearby Omnibus University. He wanted to study accounting and business management. But how could he muster the funds? With financial assistance from his family out of the question, how could he manage to pay for tuition and fees, books and supplies, housing, food, and clothes?

Having become used to substandard housing while growing up, Tim felt his prayers had been answered when he came onto an opportunity to care for research chickens every morning and afternoon in exchange for the use of one room in an outmoded university poultry facility that had been remodeled to provide minimal student housing. He prepared simple meals using an old refrigerator and hot plate to supplement leftovers the pizzeria owner gave him at clock-out time every night.

With housing and food assured, Tim turned to another major college expense – tuition and fees. Fortunately, with tuition still reasonably priced and fees almost nil in those days, proceeds of his full-time summer employment and part-time jobs at college enabled Tim to pay for these himself in monthly installments.

> Let us not look back in anger or forward in fear, but around in awareness.
>
> **James Thurber (1894-1961)**
> **American writer**

In today's higher education environment, Tim Ballew would find it difficult, if not impossible, to pay for college without borrowing money. Educational opportunities for students from low- and middle-income families have been drastically affected as the gap between college costs and available financial aid has widened alarmingly. During the 15-

year period that began in 1980, tuition at four-year public colleges in the United States increased 234% and faculty salaries 97%, but at the same time median household income increased only 82%, prices of consumer goods only 74%, and federal government student grants only 72%. Ridiculously, tuition increased over three times faster than did the federal Pell Grants, the single most important means of providing financial aid for students from low-income families, and almost three times faster than median household income.

The financial pressure on families due to exorbitant increases in tuition and fees has been exacerbated by an increasing tax burden. A family of four at median income in 1948 paid 2% of its income in taxes. In 1994, that figure was 25%. Many families wishing to see their daughters and sons attend college feel they are on a financial treadmill.

> Ye shall know the truth, and the truth shall make you sad.
>
> **Aldous L. Huxley (1894-1963)**
> **British novelist and critic**

Angela Martin was the oldest of three children. While her parents had no formal education past high school, both wanted their first-born to pursue a college degree. That was Angela's goal, too.

The Martins all worked hard, but barely scraped by financially. As an office worker at a day care center, Angela's mother – a hard-working people-person – earned the minimum wage. Mrs. Martin's health-care plan and other benefits were barebones. Angela's father – a responsible, popular individual – was unable to secure a job that provided health-care benefits. He was held back by a history of depression tracing to his military service in Vietnam as a United States Marine, as well as a lack of postsecondary education and training. Mr. Martin worked 30 hours a week as a bank guard and 30 hours as a shopping-mall security officer. When his work schedule permitted, he helped coach a church-league soccer team. From middle school on, Angela Martin worked part-time as a baby sitter. During her junior and senior years in high school, she also saved some money for college from part-time jobs at a fast-food restaurant and a floral shop.

Her peers and adults alike viewed Angela as an "all-American girl". A "happy-to-be-alive" person, always ready and willing to run errands or perform favors for a neighbor in need; an enthusiastic volunteer Candy Striper at the local hospital; a friend to all. In school, she averaged "A-" grades, wrote for the school newspaper, and was tapped for membership in the National Honor Society.

A compassionate, disciplined, responsible young woman of high integrity and strong values, Angela's upbeat personality made her easy to meet and difficult to forget, a natural for the career she had dreamed about for years – teaching. The more she thought about becoming an elementary teacher, the more intensely she wanted to emulate Miss Sparks, the caring, high-energy teacher she had admired and respected ever since second grade.

Her greatest anxiety was whether she would be able to arrange the finances needed to achieve her goal. She saved all she could, but at her low wage level, would it be enough? Her parents saved what they could, as well. But it seemed that every time their "college fund" reached a significant amount, paying medical and other bills would decimate their savings, and they would have to start all over again.

Angela Martin was thrilled by the good news of her admission to Omnibus University's College of Education. In the envelope with the acceptance letter were applications for housing in the university residence halls and for financial aid, which she promptly completed and returned. She was most anxious about money matters. She carefully listed her savings and estimated how much she expected to earn as a part-time employee at a convenience store, a job she nailed down on a visit to Collegeville. Her parents completed the financial aid form with information about their income, assets, and projected ability to support their daughter's college education. Three weeks later, a form letter advised the Martins that Angela's first semester financial-aid package was assured.

Angela Martin's first semester at Omnibus University was good and it was sad. The coursework turned her on, and she enjoyed college life. But during the same period her father experienced a serious depression resulting in a loss of work. Major health-related expenses crushed all of Angela's hope for any financial help from her family the second semester. The Martins faced the bleak reality and borrowed money from a university emergency loan fund to help with the next semester's costs.

That semester, again, things went well school-wise for Angela, but not at all well family-wise. Her father's health continued to degenerate, and by now her mother was missing work, too, in order to care for her spouse. It became clear to Angela that she could expect little or no further financial help from home.

Discouraged, Angela decided to drop out of college for a year. Living at home, she would take a full-time job at the day care center where her mother worked and a part-time job nights and weekends as a waitress. Money saved from her earnings at these jobs, she reasoned, would provide the dollars needed to pay back her emergency loans and resume her college education.

Happily, things went well that year, and in the fall Angela returned to college. Her savings during that time away plus the cash from current part-time work and financial aid from the state and federal governments were sufficient to pay for her third semester. During her fourth semester, however, Angela once again was forced to borrow from the emergency fund. Academically, things went well, though – one "A", four "Bs".

At that point, having completed just two years of college, Angela Martin again had to face realities, and she dropped out of college once again, to "save-up" for year three. Fortunately, she was able to resume both of her jobs from the year before.

Unfortunately, her plan hit a snag. Halfway through the year, she became ill and was advised that her disease, chronic nephritis, would require regular therapy for the rest of her life. More bad news was that, since she had dropped out of college and was working full-time, her mother's health insurance would no longer cover Angela's medical expenses. As a temporary employee – even though full-time – she received no health insurance benefits of her own. She was living frugally, but medical bills nearly consumed her earnings. Moreover, she had to pay back that fourth-semester emergency loan.

After weeks of reviewing her predicament – the fact that college tuition and fees were increasing much faster than her ability to earn and save, coupled with her need to pay off the debt she had already incurred – Angela Martin made a profound decision. She would put aside her determination to finish college. Instead, she would seek the sort of full-time employment that would eventually provide much-needed health insurance.

So ashamed and disappointed she could barely look at herself in the mirror, Angela's change in plans left her bitter and discouraged. She had always believed that, somehow in this land of plenty, the ambitions of a conscientious, steadfast student, one who always had served others and tried to be a model citizen, would be fulfilled. And she was astounded by newspaper articles reporting the extravagant incomes enjoyed by college coaches who cheated in recruiting student-athletes; university administrators who systematically bilked the system; and unproductive faculty members who nevertheless enjoyed the protection of life-long academic tenure.

Angela Martin would be reminded every day for the rest of her life that she had failed to achieve her goal. She would be haunted by nagging incompleteness, unfulfilled ambition. She would bear the stigma of being among the lower paid (in 1995, college graduates earned nearly 84% more than high-school graduates). She would forever fear being perceived as a failure. She would be working in less desirable environments. Her children would have fewer opportunities than many of their classmates. She would envy every day of her life those who had been privileged enough to achieve their educational goals.

A nation without the means of reform is without the means of survival.
Edmund Burke (1729-1797)
British statesman and orator

THE CONTEXT OF THE TALES

Here is the reality, plain and simple. Our ivory tower is under siege. People are questioning our mission and questioning who we are. They claim we cost too much, spend carelessly, teach poorly, plan myopically, and, when questioned, respond defensively.
Thomas H. Kean (b. 1935)
President, Drew University

American higher education is a troubled enterprise. Amid inefficient policies and practices, archaic decision-making, self-serving incentive structures, the depredations of affirmative action and political correctness, and consequent ever-rising costs, colleges and universities face monumental clientele resistance and the scorn of public officials who reflect the disapproving attitudes of the taxpaying electorate, which rightly comes to bat last.

Following almost four decades of uninterrupted growth in enrollments, facilities, programs, and popularity, higher education in the United States has become entangled in a Sargasso sea of seemingly insurmountable problems. Demographic realities, funding reductions, tuition increases, scandals in programs from athletics to research, and serious waning of public respect and support have combined to thrust new stresses on our nation's thirteenth largest business entity, an enterprise that serves 15 million students and employs 2.6 million faculty and staff in 3700 institutions with budgets totaling $160 billion a year.

Those who hope prevailing negative public opinion will abate any time soon, alas, hope in vain. These problems are anything but transitory. Public outcries about accessibility, accountability, affordability, and academic outcomes cast serious doubt on the academy's ability to manage itself at this critical time.

The question is *who*? Who will orchestrate renewal? The academy itself? Or the burgeoning, fledgling, nontraditional industry in postsecondary education that holds neither affinity with nor allegiance to institutional traditions?

Would-be reformers have viewed academic departments as professional guilds seeking to sustain individual privilege at the expense of initiatives aimed at improving teaching to enhance learning. Others portray them as clandestine cliques of arrogant, egotistical, self-appointed experts who are accountable and allegiant, first, to their individual personal agendas; second, to their academic disciplines; third (and often as an afterthought), to the institutions that provide them legitimacy, place, and service. Largely lost in this ethos is the unity that results when faculty colleagues subscribe to common goals and strategies.

> Too many people don't care what happens so long as it doesn't happen to them.
> **William Howard Taft (1857-1930)**
> **Twenty-seventh President, United States of America**

Nearly 60 percent of Americans believe higher education needs a fundamental overhaul. By a margin of roughly 8:1, the public believes college education is too expensive, not good value for the money, and quickly pricing itself out of the reach of many qualified students. Most Americans also believe that, for the good of all, the poor should not be deprived of the educational opportunities of the rich.

There abounds *dry rot in the ivory tower*. It is insidious. In the chapters that follow, I pull back the shutters and the blinds and the curtains of the ivory tower, and share anecdotes that throw light on problems in today's higher education enterprise in the United States. These problems are derivative from thousands upon thousands of occasions when often well-meaning but misguided or inherently weak individuals in positions of trust winked at the rules, abandoned fundamental values, and participated in unethical practices.

> Alike for the nation and the individual, the one indispensable requisite is character.
> **Theodore Roosevelt (1858-1914)**
> **Twenty-sixth President, United States of America**

What has been going on has been wrong, and it should not be ignored. The accumulation of these wrongs is about to bring down the ivory tower. Decreasing revenue streams and financial constraints notwithstanding, the most compelling imperative in academe today is to eradicate *dry rot in the ivory tower*. The complacency and obliviousness about all this throughout the academy is appalling.

The story line I have developed constitutes a fiction based on my observations and knowledge of situations at dozens of contemporary colleges and universities in the United States. Because of the crucial interrelatedness of such situations at any given institution, however, I have created a pseudo-institution – Omnibus University – as the setting for the parables, a device which makes it possible to explore essential complexities. Names of individuals used in this book are fictitious and the vignettes are amalgams and not meant to refer to any actual persons.

Finally, I am not merely blowing the whistle on higher education. I believe in higher education. Indeed, I am and have been myself part of higher education. But I believe higher education in this country today needs to confront its problems more vigorously. I shall tell the story as I see it, hoping that readers will be moved to do what they can to set the system aright. In the last chapter, I shall discuss ridding the ivory tower of its dry rot, by fumigation and ventilation, in order to renew the academic sanctuary.

The history of higher education is littered with grandiose blueprints for change – the debris of dozens of well-intentioned but ultimately failed efforts. But the rhetoric of reform is one of the proudest traditions of the academy.

Charles J. Sykes (b. 1954)
***ProfScam* (1988), p. 151**

Come, my friends, it is not too late to make a better world.

Alfred, Lord Tennyson (1809-1892)
English poet

CHAPTER 1

ON DRY ROT AND IVORY TOWERS

Men, like nails, lose their usefulness when they lose
direction and begin to bend.

Walter S. Landor (1775-1864)
English author

٪ A trustee called on the president of Omnibus University and
asked him to direct a dean to order a department head to suggest
to a rhetoric professor that she change a student's grade. To be
changed: a particular student's final recorded grade in a required
rhetoric course. The particular student: the daughter of a client
of the banker-trustee.

Everyone in the academic-administrative chain immediately
and obediently did as directed. Everyone, that is, except the professor. She demurred. She hesitated because, for one thing, she
believed in high academic standards. For another, in honor of
the ideal of academic freedom, she ordinarily did not follow her
departmental administrator's suggestions. At least, not right
away.

But then the dean played a trump card. He reminded the
professor that the course of her own promotion could be affected
if ultimately she were to refuse to change the grade. In the end,
the rhetoric professor, too, did what she had been asked to do.

All five university functionaries in this sorry episode let their personal and professional morals disintegrate as they conspired to break their own rules and commit this fraud, this crime against academic integrity, this outrageously unfair act. All for the silly sake of satisfying some university trustee's impudent promise to a friend that he would arrange a favor.

⅋ For more than a decade, the manager of Omnibus's emblematic merchandise store sold university property on the black market to a local merchant, keeping the cash proceeds for himself. The exchange of merchandise for a check happened openly, but for a long time no one but the two traders knew that, all along, the check's payee was the manager himself!

One day, the manager was unexpectedly called away from the store at the wrong time. Just long enough for his black-market customer to take another load of goods and leave another check on the manager's desk. In the process, the assistant manager discovered the scam, which a sting operation confirmed.

The long-time store manager was required to make partial restitution to the university and to resign. But university officials did not turn the evidence over to law-enforcement authorities, so criminal charges were never brought against him.

Hence, several officials – primarily in order to preserve their own reputations, for this massive theft of university property over many years had happened on their watch – conspired with one another as they feloniously covered-up the employee's larceny.

⅋ The Omnibus Octopi coach was desperate the early May afternoon when he begged the athletic director to find a way to keep a student-athlete academically eligible to play football the next fall. In over twenty years at the helm of Octopus athletics, the clever, well-connected athletic director had always "found a way". This case would be no exception.

The athletic director deftly arranged for the young man to receive transfer credit on his official Omnibus academic record for a phantom algebra course at a remote community college. The "student" played football that fall, all right. But he had allowed himself to be led astray. He had conspired with the athletic director, the football coach, registrars' office personnel at both institutions, and others, in perpetrating this fraud. Their actions stemmed from arrogance, from disrespect for university policies, for National Collegiate Athletic Association rules, for common decency.

◢ ◢ ◢

Dry Rot: Decay from within caused especially by resistance to new forces.

Ivory Tower: An impractical often escapist attitude marked by aloof lack of concern with or interest in practical matters or urgent problems.

Merriam-Webster's Collegiate Dictionary
Tenth Edition, 1998

The overwhelming debacle that today besets colleges and universities all across the United States both reflects and derives from *dry rot in the ivory tower*. This pervasive malady – now running rampant in the nation's higher educational system – has resulted mainly from institutional leadership inadequate for these dynamic times.

He who rejects change is the architect of decay.

James Harold Wilson (b. 1916)
Prime Minister, United Kingdom
(1964-1970; 1974-1976)

Institutions of higher education that once enjoyed the public's unflagging admiration, confidence, and loyalty have created instead an educational marketplace where a strong admonition prevails: caveat emptor. Increasingly as time goes on, higher education's customers – the students, their sponsors, and their eventual employers – believe not only that a college education is too expensive – but also that universities "cost too much, spend carelessly, teach poorly, plan myopically, and, when questioned, respond defensively".

Universities need to improve the quality of their services to students; the nature of their accountability to taxpayers; the depth of their commitment to excellence. (This goes for private institutions as well as public ones; with but a handful of exceptions, taxpayers subsidize every institution of higher education in this nation.) Instead, incredibly, this nation's universities continue to demonstrate an enduring passion for special consideration and privilege, with job preservation invariably turning out to be job one.

> Left totally on its own, the university will evolve toward self-interest rather than public interest.
>
> **Frank C. Newman (b. 1917)**
> **American legal educator**

The American citizenry criticizes our universities as never before. It finds them choking from the burdens of bureaucracy – paperwork and permits, confusion and delays, double-talk and run-arounds, buck-passing, red-taping. It perceives academics as extolling narrow scholarly disciplines instead of excellent educational services. It concludes that these overpaid, out-of-touch whiners teach and counsel students too little, conduct research and private consultation too much.

For their parts, many faculty members naively trust that students will always eagerly flock to their classrooms; that legislators will always enthusiastically and unquestioningly support their programs; that individuals, corporations, and foundations will eagerly wait in queue for the chance to invest their earnings and savings, their profits and inheritances, in the professors' scholarly endeavors.

These same faculty members view productive intercourse with the public as sometimes a strategic necessity rather than always a natural adjunct to their work. Such a haplessly reactive mindset needs to be replaced by a proactive educational environment where student success, scholarly excellence, and genuine public service comprise the prime institutional objectives.

Those of us concerned about this current state of affairs must make no mistake. The challenges facing higher education in the United States today are neither negligible nor transitory. Serious issues abound: access, accountability, affordability, efficiency, outcomes, productivity, quality, to mention a few among many. They give parents and politicians and pundits – not to mention pupils – ample reason to question the essence of today's academic enterprise. And it seems as if everyone has taken full advantage of every opportunity to raise such questions.

> If there is anything education does not lack today, it is critics.
>
> **Nathan M. Pusey (b. 1907)**
> **President, Harvard University (1953-1971)**

So far, academe's responses have been pitifully ineffectual. Predictably, then, tangible public support for higher education has been on the wane in recent years. In California, for example, the proportion of state-appropriated dollars going to support the higher education system decreased from 13 percent in 1990 to 9 percent in 1995 (while that for the corrections system increased from 4 percent to 8 percent).

The current, sad condition of America's universities was characterized in 1993 by the Wingspread Group on Higher Education:[1]

> A disturbing and dangerous mismatch exists between what American society needs of higher education and what it is receiving. Nowhere is the mismatch more dangerous than in the quality of undergraduate preparation provided on many campuses. The American imperative for the twenty-first century is that society must hold higher education to much higher expectations or risk national decline ... . The withdrawal of public support for higher education can only

accelerate as students, parents, and taxpayers come to understand that they paid for an expensive education without receiving fair value in return ... . The 3400^2 institutions of higher education in America come in all shapes and sizes, public and private ... . Despite this diversity, most operate as though their focus were still the traditional student of days gone by: a white, male, recent high school graduate, who attended classes full-time at a four-year institution and lived on campus. Yesterday's traditional student is, in fact, today's exception.

What does society need from higher education? It needs stronger, more vital forms of community. It needs an informed and involved citizenry. It needs graduates able to assume leadership roles in American life. It needs a competent and adaptable workforce. It needs very high quality undergraduate education producing graduates who can sustain each of these goals. It needs more first-rate research pushing back the important boundaries of human knowledge and less research designed to lengthen academic resumes. It needs an affordable, cost-effective educational enterprise offering lifelong learning. Above all, it needs a commitment to the American promise – the idea that all Americans have the opportunity to develop their talents to the fullest.

Alas, and ironically, universities have been turned into bastions of conservatism. Even the suggestion of a need for adaptive change typically evokes strong resistance within the academy, change being viewed as something to be avoided or, failing that, to be attacked, neutralized, and expelled. The structures of academic institutions have evolved so they resist change, not encourage, foment, and support it.

Of course, it is nearly impossible to effect change where the conventional notion has it that there is little or no need for change; where smug self-satisfaction reigns; where status quo enjoys reverence. More and more, those who inhabit higher education's ivory tower are unlikely of their own volition to ask whether a policy should be changed; to turn off a program; to shut down a unit. By ignoring the obvious, of course, they are encouraging *dry rot*.

Most ailing organizations have developed a functional blindness to their own defects. They are not suffering because they cannot solve their problems, but because they cannot see their problems.

John W. Gardner (b. 1912)
Past President, Carnegie Foundation
Former U. S. Secretary of Health, Education and Welfare
American author and founder of Common Cause

Two controversial professorial entitlements – academic freedom and academic tenure – rightly arose in another place and time to protect the professoriate against abuses from outside academe. But lately academic freedom and academic tenure have been called upon – shamelessly or shamefully, depending on one's point of view – to serve as sturdy crossbeams supporting status quo. Paradoxically, these once justifiable, utterly necessary tenets have come to provide much of the internal resistance that has led to deadly *dry rot.*

Furthermore, each member of the academic community conceptualizes his or her own role very personally, and therefore – being based on unique individual experiences – as differing from all others. This reality makes fruitful efforts by academic teams involving more than a couple of professors unusual. Even when larger groups – a department, a college, a university faculty, for example – try to make music, as occasionally they do for a time, alas, they can not. As each individual professor loudly and proudly reads from his very own special page in the songbook, the result is cacophony, not symphony.

But the real tragedy in America's educational ivory tower today has to do with the decline in leadership at all levels. Nowadays, to move an academic unit from a position of mediocrity to one of distinction – or even to maintain an institution's level of excellence – requires nothing less than heroic, statesmanlike leadership.

Much of what commonly passes as leadership – conspicuous position-taking without followers or follow-through, posturing on various public stages, manipulation without general purpose, authoritarianism – is no more leadership than the behavior of small boys marching in front of a parade, who continue to strut along Main Street after the procession has turned down a side street toward the fairgrounds.

James McGregor Burns

Individuals not prone to select the safe road of status quo – those willing to assume their common-sense and ethical responsibilities to point out the problems and opportunities, things that could and should be improved – can expect to be challenged, misinterpreted, misquoted and to serve as the butt of calumnies within the academy. Quite often these days, rocking the boat has resulted in the rocker's being abruptly and unceremoniously tossed overboard. And all this typically happens without the accused having the benefit of one's ordinary constitutional right to face his accuser.

Many of today's university leaders seem to have lost touch with the fundamental mission of higher education in our democratic culture.[3] Oh, the words are there. But, in more cases than not, the impassioned commitment is not.

In many cases genuine commitment has been replaced by arrogant, egotistical, selfish abrogation of a leader's tacit responsibility to lead in bold, decisive, yet statesmanlike fashion. Too many of today's administrators in higher education lack the courage, the feel, the persistence, the selflessness, the vision that stand as hallmarks of powerful leadership.

Sometimes this is because a person is simply a misfit, the individual's electors having set him up (often unwittingly) to confirm The Peter Principle.[4] At one level of consciousness or another he eventually recognizes his unfitness, and consequently then lacks sufficient self-confidence to effectively carry out his duties. Moreover, he then often attempts to compensate by becoming a consummate master of ephemeralities, etherealities, and esoterica in terms of guiding philosophy, and of malfeasance and even fraud and felony in terms of operations management.

Vacillating people seldom succeed. They seldom win the solid respect of their fellows. Successful men and women are very careful in reaching decisions and very persistent and determined in action thereafter.

L. G. Elliott

The need for fundamental change within the ivied *ivory tower* has been relished about as much as thoughts of root-canal therapy. Anticipation of the pain associated with the remedy undoubtedly explains much of the inertia within the academic establishment. With a diseased tooth, for example, the pain eventually becomes so excruciating that one orders the procedure that will bring relief. Despite the painful treatment, on balance, the patient knows he will be better off for having been treated.

In higher education, the pain of distrust-related reductions in appropriated public money has often been significant and sometimes even critical. But in general it has not yet been severe enough to provoke widespread calls from within the academy for the fundamental changes that will be necessary in the end. Unless and until more serious crises come along, some universities probably will continue to neglect the clear need for change. Many *ivory-tower* institutions that fail to prepare for the twenty-first century by reacting in a thoroughly adaptive mode will succumb to terminal *dry rot*.

ॐ ॐ ॐ

In the meantime, "Enough is enough already." The foul rate is so high that this game is apt to run amok, to run out of control. The whistle needs to be blown more often.

In this book, I blow the whistle on a few of the outrageous anomalies I have observed and have knowledge of in contemporary universities all across the land. Whereas episodes such as those related on succeeding pages used to be exceptional, they are now more the rule.

Blowing the whistle gives me neither comfort nor joy. Moreover, I blow the whistle not because I think I have better powers of perception and deduction than anyone else.

Discontent is the first step in the progress of a man or a
nation.

Oscar F. Wilde (1854-1900)
Irish playwright

From conversations with numerous peers from all over the
country, it is clear that most academicians know about these
anomalies. Many find them – as I do – outrageous and unaccept-
able. These peers' discontent has confirmed mine, and this in
turn has encouraged me to take the second step.

We are not afraid to follow truth wherever it may lead,
nor to tolerate any error so long as reason is left free to
combat it.

Thomas Jefferson (1743-1826)
Third President, United States of America

So, I blow the whistle because I see widespread yearnings
among academicians that our higher education system be extri-
cated from the mucky ditch in which it is mired and placed again
on the terra firma of the high road, where it used to be and
should have been all along.

Stand with those who stand right. Part with those who
go wrong ... . Let us have faith that right makes might, and in
that faith let us to the end dare to do our duty as we
understand it.

Abraham Lincoln (1809-1865)
Sixteenth President, United States of America

---

[1]*An American Imperative: Higher Expectations for Higher Education*,
Report of the Wingspread Group on Higher Education, The Johnson
Foundation, Inc., Racine, WI, 1993
[2]An estimated 3706 in 1996. National Center for Education Statistics,
Washington, DC
[3]*Reclaiming a Lost Heritage: Land-Grant and Other Higher Education Initiatives for the Twenty-First Century*, Campbell, John R.,
Michigan State University Press, East Lansing, MI, 1998
[4]*The Peter Principle: Why Things Always Go Wrong*, Peter, Laurence J.
and Raymond Hull, William Morrow, New York, 1969

REMEMBERING ... *The Tales of Two Students*

Policy shifts by the federal and state governments, and by colleges themselves, have combined with demographic transitions to create a growing population of "have nots": students whose college choices are severely limited by money. They are sometimes shut out of the most-prestigious institutions, and in many cases the institution that would be best for them .... Across the country, people who watch enrollment trends say the neediest students are enrolling in community colleges in largest numbers – or are not going to college at all.

Stephen Burd, Patrick Healy, Kit Lively, and Christopher Shea
"Low-Income Students Say Their College Options Are Limited"
The Chronicle of Higher Education, **June 14, 1996, p. A10**

The passing of the industrial age and the coming of the information age have created extraordinary changes in the economy and sometimes disruptive changes to the nation's workforce. For many Americans, the nature of work has changed, and with it, the skills and knowledge needed to be successful in the workplace. And there is growing recognition that education and training are inextricably linked to employment opportunities and economic well-being.

Esther M. Rodriguez and Sandra S. Ruppert, *Post Secondary*
Education and the New Workforce, **State Higher Education**
Executive Officers, Denver, CO, October 1996

Tuition at four-year public colleges has risen nearly three times as much as median household income over the past 15 years, according to the General Accounting Office. Between academic 1980-81 and 1994-95, tuition increased 234 percent ...

Lisa Guernsey, "Tuition Costs Continue to Outpace Median Incomes"
The Chronicle of Higher Education, **September 6, 1996, p. A59**

The bill for college freshman Melissa Drozd of Harwood Heights, Illinois, prompted the following statement from Mariann Drozd, Melissa's mother, "It's overwhelming. I had always known it was going to be expensive, but when you actually see the numbers, it is a little bit of a shock."

"College Costs Going Higher ... College Fees Rising Faster
Than Inflation", *Chicago Sun-Times*, **May 27, 1997, pp. 1-2**

... [T]he lower in-state tuition, the more likely high school graduates will stay home to attend college.

Where Have All the Students Gone?
Interstate Migration of Recent Science and Engineering Graduates
Southern Technology Council, Triangle Park, NC
February 1998, p. 20

CHAPTER 2

GOVERNING BOARDS
THAT DO NOT GOVERN

> Duty is the sublimest word in our language. Do your
> duty in all things. You cannot do more. You should never
> wish to do less.
>
> **Robert E. Lee (1807-1870)**
> **American Confederate general**

As Mary Ruth Fahey was growing up on a working farm, she spent many hours every week reading – novels, biographies, newsmagazines. And she became upset by what she learned about the status of health care for Native Americans. Her concern, fed by a television documentary, crystallized the week that Mary Ruth's church youth group spent repairing the chapel at an Arizona reservation. In those few days, she became a close friend of several of the Navajo families living there.

En route to earning three degrees at her home state's flagship public university – Omnibus University – Mary Ruth Fahey authored and saw published one book and three essays. One piece caught the public's eye when it was featured in *Parade*. Her doctoral research in political science focused on the federal health-care program for children living on reservations such as the one she first visited as a teenager. Some of her resource material came from her yearly return visits. But she depended more on the university library. Through its interlibrary loan service, she had quick access to the holdings of hundreds of academic libraries all over the country.

Upon leaving Omnibus, Fahey stayed in Collegeville, where she hung out her shingle as a freelance consultant on health-care services for the needy. Her passion for the plight of Native Americans deepened. Knowing that the fate of public-health programs rests with the political process, she plunged into a demanding avocation: statewide partisan politics.

Within three years, the man in whose gubernatorial campaign Fahey had worked so early and so hard was inaugurated governor. When the new governor appointed her to the governing board of her alma mater, she became the youngest trustee in Omnibus history.

Fahey took seriously her position on the Omnibus board, and soon developed a second passion. She worked closely with university president Benjamin Hibbard and information services dean Bonita Kroom to evaluate the university library and project future needs for information services. They estimated the extra funds the library would need to reverse a decades-long trend of purchasing fewer books and periodicals each successive year, as well as other needs: more study carrels, longer hours, enlarged databases, upgraded computer networks.

Before long, the university library had in trustee Fahey an informed and well-connected friend, able and willing to work through the political process to bring about the changes needed to ensure that Omnibus University would have top-notch, state-of-the-art information services – the fundamental infrastructure of any educational institution.

The first action step came when the board decided to place information-materials acquisitions at the top of the university's needs priorities. Then a fund-raising campaign came in over goal and before deadline, garnering matching funds from the state legislature to boot.

℘ ℘ ℘

The trouble is, most Omnibus trustees do not very much resemble trustee Mary Ruth Fahey. When they accepted a position on the board, most had something in mind other than selflessly overseeing the governance of an educational institution. They wanted power, perks, preening rights, and special privileges.

Take, for example, Malcomb Russell, an Omnibus alumnus and fourth-generation funeral director in the capital city. For thirtysome years, his close friends will say, he has resented not having high enough grades after his sophomore year to continue on the pre-medicine track, where his heart really lay. Reluctantly, at the beginning of his junior year, Russell switched to majoring in mortuary science. Some will say his anger over perceived slights by professors lies at the heart of what drives Malcomb Russell's behavior as a trustee.

Russell's family legacy has provided him financial resources and the influence they command, as well as the necessary network of contacts, that have enabled him to achieve being appointed by governors, Democrats and Republicans alike, to three consecutive seven-year terms on the Omnibus University board of trustees.

As time has passed, trustee Russell – who nowadays refers to himself, with a wink, as "the trustees' trustee" – knows a lot about what makes Omnibus tick, and he meddles much in the institution's day-to-day operations. He has been integrally involved in the appointment of three presidents in a row, and – remarkably – scores of vice-presidents, deans, and directors, and – more remarkably – hundreds of faculty and staff members. Unfortunately, his selections usually are not based on academic or professional merits.

Most of these initiatives have been self-imposed tasks, and to say Malcomb Russell has relished them would be to understate the case. In one noteworthy instance, a fellow trustee who was in favor of a presidential candidate not favored by Russell ended his laudatory comments by opining that, if the candidate were to come to Omnibus, everyone in the university family would have to "either saddle-up or be left breathing the dust". At this point, the trustees' trustee interjected a squelcher of a rhetorical question, "And what if the university family doesn't *want* to saddle-up?"

As is common practice in academe, Omnibus administrators send their recommendations on personnel actions, major purchases, and other important matters to each trustee at least a week before a board meeting. For his part, Russell carefully reviews every proposal, and invariably he is soon on the telephone discussing them – one by one – with the president. So far, the trustees' trustee has intimidated every president he has dealt with.

Over the years, trustee Russell has exercised *de facto* unilateral veto power over matters of all sorts, usually making a substitute proposal more to his taste. For many years, as a self-appointed committee of one, he has set the salaries for individual administrators and key faculty and staff members. In the process, the trustees' trustee, whose memory for petty gossip and perceived slights is akin to that of the proverbial elephant bull, can display a revengeful spirit akin to that of the proverbial playground bully.

Russell's antics have caused problems for four Omnibus presidents as they have tried to work with search committees, promotion and tenure committees, courses and curricula committees, and line and staff administrators carrying all sorts of portfolios. For one thing, savvy external individuals and organizations now lobby trustee Russell directly on behalf of their own special agendas, providing heady experiences for the trustees' trustee. He encourages the practice of entreating his support through bowing and scraping in his direction, mostly by seeing to it that his selfish wishes become board actions and policies.

Truth be told, though, Russell could not hold such sway if his fellow trustees put their collective foot down. His colleagues' abrogation of responsibility – as they mumly sit by and tacitly permit the outrageous behavior that is the signature of the trustees' trustee – has left its indelible mark on the university.

It is neither a positive mark nor a proud one. Although the trustees' trustee is feared by most in the university family, he is admired and respected by few. And as news of this one man's reputation for interference has spread on grapevines that cross state lines, the university's ability to attract and retain strong talent to its faculty and administration has been damaged. The culture of Omnibus is in many ways the poorer for the trustees' trustee having been permitted by his irresponsible colleagues to have such a heavy hand in its governance for nearly two decades.

Trustee Russell's stranglehold on Omnibus business is being challenged of late, though. For example, the library project is nowhere near the top of the trustees' trustee's priority list. But trustee Mary Ruth Fahey's straightforward, well-developed, highly publicized initiatives so far have proved difficult for him to control, let alone smother.

And also, several years ago, Frank Drysdale, an Omnibus alumnus and dentist practicing in a county seat town 70 miles northeast of Collegeville, worked hard and finally managed to gain a coveted gubernatorial appointment to the Omnibus board. All along, he has had but one item on his agenda: to do what he can to tilt the focus of the institution – with strong traditions in agriculture, engineering, the arts, and the humanities – so it could become a center of excellence in biomedical research. His approach to pushing his agenda would be to jockey himself into a position that would enable him to strongly influence the next choice for university president, then to see to it that the new leader shared his revolutionary view and had the moxie to pull off the revolution.

Although Drysdale successfully politicked for a place on the next president search and selection committee, he was still naive on one front. He did not appreciate the clout the trustees' trustee would have even from outside the committee.

Trustee Drysdale was disgusted when the committee ultimately recommended, and the full board concurred "unanimously", that Burton Cromley – trustee Russell's favorite candidate, an Omnibus alumnus, a former civil engineering professor at Omnibus University who most recently had served as a research administrator in private industry – be the next chief executive.

The day Cromley was inaugurated president was not a happy one for Drysdale. He was determined to work all the harder to have a like-minded individual sitting in the president's office. "Next time!" became his unmuffled, oft-uttered promise.

Of course, for the time being, Omnibus University did not need a new president. Ever the stubborn optimist when it came to his fixations, though, Drysdale saw the situation as both challenge and opportunity. He simply repositioned himself on the gameboard to start-minus-one. Before he could start anew seeking a president more to his liking, he had to arrange for the incumbent to be dumped. So he energetically and intently set himself to thoroughly undermining president Cromley. His strategy: to develop a mountain of evidence in support of his long-held contention that Burton Cromley was the wrong person for the job.

Trustee Drysdale approached his new task by taking his cue from Page One in trustee Russell's play book. As soon as Drysdale received his package of administration recommendations prior to a board meeting, he did his homework. Then, at the board meeting, he would act assertively, appearing to less energetic fellow trustees to be analytical and well-informed. Over the months, this set the stage for Drysdale's often successful cajoling of a majority of the board to see things his way. He dealt largely with a big bag of tidbits of gossip and innuendo. But several trustees soon showed their vulnerability to these petty points.

b b b

A year or so into Drysdale's get-Cromley campaign, several opportunities to enhance his power base on the board were laid in his lap, and he seized them. In one notorious case, the application by the son of a strong supporter of the governor to attend law school at Omnibus was rejected. The applicant's father called the governor, who gladly obliged by calling trustee Frank Drysdale, whom he had only recently appointed to the board. The governor emphasized the "importance" of this particular young man's being admitted to the Omnibus University College of Law. He could have contacted the board chair, Kristina Papazaglou. But she was a member of a different political party, and the governor had had only mediocre success gaining favors from her.

Drysdale arranged to visit Cromley at the president's residence the very same evening. With no lead-up, he laid out his case, and then just as abruptly ended the brief conversation by ordering the president to "do whatever is necessary to effect the admission", to "do it right away", and to "call me immediately when the matter has been taken care of ".

Although the president was not required to follow the unilateral directive of an individual trustee, he already had been stung more than once when he ignored such orders. So early the next morning, Cromley had a teleconference with then law dean Thorsson Kehrberg. The president explained the situation, reminding the dean that – in view of the several special requests that invariably came in each year – he had earlier recommended reserving a few admission slots for "special cases".

Such an approach would cause serious problems in the law college, dean Kehrberg argued. The faculty had developed a comprehensive approach to evaluating applicants, based on pre-law grades, aptitude-test scores, letters of recommendation, and interview results. He added that hundreds of students had faithfully studied for years preparing for this competitive admission process, and that he always advocated employing the ethical principles of fairness and integrity. It turned out that, in this particular case, the applicant's grades and aptitude-test scores placed the young man in the lowest quartile of applicants, well below the cut-off line. The dean wanted to know, "How can I, in good conscience, go to the admission committee and ask for an exception here? There comes a time when we should just straightaway say, 'No'."

The president listened to the dean, said little, agreed to meet again right after lunch.

At the early afternoon meeting, the dean opened by telling the president that he simply could not honor this special request for admission, even if it did originate with the governor. The president swiveled his chair around, looked out the window behind his desk a few moments, turned back to face the dean and said, "I guess this is just one of those times a fellow needs to ease up on his principles."

Dean Kehrberg stood up. "I get your message," he said. "My resignation, effective 5 p.m. today, will be on your desk within the hour."

> To see what is right and not to do it is want of courage.
> **Confucius (551-479 BC)**
> **Chinese philosopher**

𝒮 𝒮 𝒮

Another case in which trustee Drysdale injected himself – again on behalf of the governor, who was responding this time to a request from the United States Department of State – involved an engineering student who hailed from a developing nation on the Pacific Rim and Dr. Cara McInerny, an assistant professor of electrical engineering at Omnibus. The young faculty member had already demonstrated her superb skills as both teacher and researcher.

One day, as students were completing their final examination in professor McInerny's course on superconductivity, she watched carefully as one student – whom she had come to know as a personable young man – was copying answers from the test booklet of a top achiever seated next to him. The professor asked her examination proctors to observe the scene, and all agreed that the student was flagrantly cheating.

McInerny had emphasized in the first class meeting of the semester that any student found cheating would fail the course. So she had no choice but to advise the student, when he turned in his test booklet, that he had been observed breaking a university rule and would receive an "F" grade. The student seemed to be unshaken as he nonchalantly told her he had enjoyed the course and left the room.

Before registering the grades for the course, McInerny conferred with the head of electrical engineering, who – based on the information provided – concurred with the professor's decision and promised to support it.

About a week later, repercussion surfaced. The student happened to be the son of an influential family in his home country. In the wake of the incident, his father hastily scheduled a meeting with the United States consul to that country, who immediately filed a report with the Department of State in Washington. The next day, the undersecretary of state telephoned the governor and asked him to investigate the matter and get back with him. "You have to know," he told the governor, "that this kid's family can hurt American software exports to that country in a big way."

The governor once again turned to trustee Frank Drysdale. When the trustee called on the president this time, he told him, "Do whatever it takes to bring this case to favorable resolution. The governor and the State Department are watching." He added that, as a trustee, he was "embarrassed by this McInerny's lack of sensitivity in going ahead and assigning an "F" to an international student for *allegedly* cheating".

Cromley resented Drysdale's quick willingness to believe the student, criticize the professor, and accede to the governor's request that he involve himself in the matter. But he realized, too, that he had many seemingly more important board matters with which to deal. So with an assistant he arranged an approach to bring about that "favorable resolution". He called the dean of engineering, laid out the problem, and asked him to come to the president's office for a conference, bringing along the professor and her department head. He also asked the dean to call prior to the meeting to advise the president on what he would be proposing.

Dean Hilton Herberger never questioned a request from the president. In this case, he easily decided to use the promotion and tenure process as a hammer on Cara McInerny. On short notice, he called her and the department head to his office. When they arrived, he handed them a memorandum addressed to the professor: "We have been pleased with your research and your teaching. Both have reflected well on this college and Omnibus University. As you know, you soon will be coming up for promotion to associate professor with tenure. Ordinarily, there would be little question as to the outcome of deliberations in your case. But recent developments in the case of [here the student was named] have provoked questions by the board of trustees, the governor, and the United States Department of State. You are advised to revisit your decision to assign a failing grade to this student for an alleged infraction of the university's rules concerning irregularities in completing an examination instrument. I would further recommend that you devise a method of enabling this student to re-take the final examination in your course on superconductivity."

McInerny was deeply disappointed and disillusioned by the president's and the dean's willingness to compromise academic integrity in the face of pressure from the outside. She exchanged momentary glances with her department administrator, started to feel nauseous, and wanted to resign right then and there. But she was a single parent with two children to support; she had earned the right of passage to a tenured associate professorship; she greatly enjoyed her teaching as well as her research at Omnibus; and the market for engineering professors had become a buyer's market. So, although feeling anger and disgust and reluctance, she waffled.

Incidentally, when trustee Mary Ruth Fahey learned of this episode, she called the governor to express her surprise at his role in a plan that ignored a policy rightly set by the university faculty. The governor chuckled. "Mary Ruth, there probably are a few political realities you didn't learn about in your political science courses." Never again would Mary Ruth Fahey have as much confidence in the governor as before.

And as for trustee Malcomb Russell, upon catching wind of what had happened, he was overheard mumbling to his coffee cup, "Why didn't the governor call me?"

> I cannot give you the formula for success. But I can give you the formula for failure: Try to please everyone.
> **Herbert B. Swope (1882-1958)**
> **American author**

⊘ ⊘ ⊘

In another infamous case, for several months, trustee Frank Drysdale had been casually calling the Octopus football coach, George Peek – "just to chat, if you have a minute" – at least once a week. On one occasion, the coach gained the trustee's prior support on a matter that had serious implications for academic policy, the domain of the faculty.

The story began to unfold when provost Lucinda Howard, the university's chief academic officer, advised president Cromley that Dale Davidson – an all-conference linebacker in his third year and already being touted as a likely All-American his fourth year – had an academic problem. He had failed college algebra six times, even though three failures was the maximum allowed by university policy. Under NCAA rules, Davidson needed the credit for this course to be eligible to play intercollegiate football. The provost told the president that the board was upset and that the coach thought "there must be some way around this mess".

Cromley asked Howard why he was learning about the trustees' opinion from someone other than the trustees. She shrugged, pursed her lips, shook her head.

Coach Peek had already contacted academic coordinator for athletes Alan Bogue and, exaggerating, told him that the trustees wanted Bogue to "dig deeper" into university policy and resolve the matter. Bogue reminded Peek that university policy had already been stretched when Dale Davidson had been permitted to enroll in college algebra the fourth time, let alone the fifth and sixth times. The coach, emboldened by Drysdale's support, told Bogue, "You heard me."

With that kind of pressure, Bogue discussed the matter with the provost, who promptly informed the president. Unbeknownst to the provost, though, Drysdale had unilaterally met with the university's chief legal counsel, Richard Nailer, to review relevant university policy. Nailer – a four-letter halfback during his own Omnibus days – soon devised a workable approach: Conduct a series of tests to determine if Dale Davidson had a learning disability. If so, he would be in a special academic category and new rules would apply.

An ecstatic Drysdale immediately shared the good news with Peek, who directed Bogue to arrange the tests. Bogue would conform, but not before informing Howard.

President Cromley decided to telephone trustee Drysdale to discuss the entire matter. The conversation was to the point. The trustee interrupted the president mid-second-sentence and unilaterally directed him to move quickly on the Davidson case so the "student" would be eligible to play football come fall.

No one was surprised that Davidson was found to be learning-disabled. He would enroll in the course in college algebra for an unprecedented seventh time. With intense tutoring and an understanding instructor, Davidson received the lowest passing grade. A way around his dilemma – at one time seemingly insurmountable – had been found. Prospective All-American linebacker Dale Davidson would be an Omnibus Octopus on the gridiron for one more season.

Although none of this business came before the board of trustees for either information or action, word of it leaked out. Regardless of the beliefs and values of most trustees, power politics on the part of a handful of individual trustees was shaping Omnibus University's *de facto* policies. For one trustee – who along with Mary Ruth Fahey and a couple of others had been frustrated in unsuccessful attempts to squelch Russell's and Drysdale's nefarious antics – this episode was the last straw. He abruptly resigned from the board. In so doing, of course, he abrogated his responsibility to blow the whistle.

Drysdale was unabashed and undeterred by the incident. He capitalized on it by swiftly winning an ally in the replacement trustee. From the start, the new trustee, Cutter Humpherys, conspired with Drysdale to hamper president Cromley's attempts to effect a new tilt at Omnibus: emphasizing academics and scholarship, de-emphasizing intercollegiate athletics.

Humpherys would go along with Drysdale on matters such as presidential picks if Drysdale would go along with Humpherys on intercollegiate-athletic matters. Both trustees would talk up educational values to the media as well as Omnibus administrators, faculty, and students. But they stalwartly supported Omnibus excellence in athletics and biomedical research.

☨ ☨ ☨

Sallie Snell-Schumacher was another trustee who easily came under Frank Drysdale's influence. Sallie was the third member of her family to hold what she was fond of referring to as "the Snell seat" on the board, and she was openly proud of that legacy.

Trustee Sallie Snell-Schumacher's pet mission was to make certain that long-termers on the Omnibus staff were kept on the payroll as long as they wished. She cherished the inbreeding so evident at Omnibus. Cronyism and nepotism gave her obvious comfort. "He's been one of us for a long time, and my dad knew him well, and it's a pretty sorry hen that doesn't stick up for her chicks, and that's all there is to it," is what she had to say on many a personnel matter. Drysdale aided Snell-Schumacher in her mission by seconding her every motion related to personnel. In return, she gave him her proxy in the next presidential search.

ℒ ℒ ℒ

Spurred by a series of successes in efforts to discredit president Cromley, trustee Drysdale soon added media leaks to his tool box. He sensed that the president's penchant for recognizing Omnibus's plethora of problems and vigorously proceeding to solve them virtually always opened the chief executive to strong criticism from many in the university community who – for various, typically selfish reasons – favored *status quo.*

Many of these disgruntled individuals turned out to be wellsprings of defamatory – albeit often unfounded – gossip about Cromley. Soon Drysdale introduced evening hours in his dental practice so he could spend what turned out to be dozens of daytime hours each month on the scene at Omnibus, "getting in touch". He was pumping people for rumors that the president had said something – anything – suggesting that he had recognized a problem and intended to resolve it, of course needing to rough up *status quo* in the process.

Media folks started contacting Drysdale frequently, and it was a poorly kept secret that the dentist-trustee often was the anonymous tipster – the "informed source close to the board" – to whom insider viewpoints often were being attributed.

Far from being a constructive force for good, Frank Drysdale – in a matter of two years – had become a powerful Omnibus trustee who was set, not on statesmanly decisions honoring the best interests of the university, but rather on seeing his own far-fetched agenda come to reality.

Soon, trustee Drysdale was rewarded. After only three years at the helm of Omnibus University, beleaguered president Burton Cromley jumped out of an early-retirement window opened for all state employees by the legislature. At this point, trustee Mary Ruth Fahey reached the end of her rope, too, and prematurely announced that she would not be available for appointment to a second seven-year term.

Standing in the middle of the road is dangerous. You can get knocked down by the traffic from both sides.
Lady Margaret H. Thatcher (b. 1925)
Prime Minister, United Kingdom (1979-1990)

ℒ ℒ ℒ

By now, you may be thinking, in the "I'll-let-you-do-your-thing-if-you'll-let-me-do-mine" climate so prevalent in university governing board rooms these days, there seem to be no bounds to crassness. For most of his seven-year term as an Omnibus trustee, however, the uncouth Dr. Iain Liggett often came close to finding the limits of common decency.

Driving home after work one evening in his seventeenth year as a professor of turf-grass management at Omnibus, a new personal goal took life: Iain Liggett decided to finagle as necessary to gain a seat on the Omnibus University board of trustees. After all, he rationalized, if the trustees had their own trustee, why not the professors?

During the next two years, as part of his get-a-seat plan, Iain Liggett made several multi-thousand-dollar contributions to the university's annual foundation and general fund-raising campaigns. And he participated in hundreds of tailgate parties, open houses, receptions, stuffed-chicken-breast banquets, and cash-bar cocktail hours, not to mention countless, seemingly endless telephone conversations.

When his wife raised an eyebrow over the time, energy, and moola he was throwing the university's way, Liggett said, "This is strictly business, dear. It'll pay off in the end. You're in my will. I have some ideas. Just wait and see."

To make a long story short – much to the consternation of the aging Malcomb Russell, the trustees' trustee – the ambitiously ostentatious Dr. Iain Liggett succeeded in his quest, making history as the first faculty member to sit on the Omnibus board.

For a while there was parking-lot chatter among trustees of the likes of Russell and Drysdale about having to start pulling punches when discussing faculty matters "now that Liggett's on board". But that talk soon died down, partly because Liggett himself seemed so unconcerned about the general state-of-being of the Omnibus faculty. Indeed, although the professors' trustee would drone on about most agenda items, the chair had to intentionally pull him into discussions of any matter dealing directly with the faculty. Truth be told, Liggett was anything *but* the professors' trustee.

Also of interest: there was nary a whisper about the conflict of interest his voting membership on the board often represented, and over his seven-year term he was never asked to recuse himself from a board vote.

In the annals of the nation's higher academy, the seating of Iain Liggett as an Omnibus trustee was very strange. But some things he did – and got away with – took strangeness to a new level. Some naive members of the university community, upon hearing about the professors' trustee's antics, found the renditions incredible, in terms of his behaving in those ways as well as the fact his fellow board members sat mumly by, letting the ridiculous scenarios play out.

For example, within a year of taking his seat, Dr. Liggett and two of his associates finished developing a line of long-lasting, all-in-one lawn-care products. For the next decade, these revolutionary products would – by combining appropriate fertilizers, herbicides, and insecticides for particular applications in one bag, to be sprayed on the grass once a year – dominate the nation's lawn- and turf-care product market, resulting in billions of dollars in sales.

In fact, theirs *was* a fantastic feat. Their combination of processes made it possible to mix together as many as eleven inorganic and organic compounds, and keep the mixtures on the shelf for years, without diminishing any constituent's potency. The product line proved to be a substitute gold mine for those who held claim to the processes.

Ordinarily, Omnibus University keeps the patent rights to inventions arising from work conducted in university-sponsored projects. The inventor initiates the process by submitting a disclosure to the university's office of patents and intellectual properties, which decides whether to seek a patent. If a patent is granted, as an incentive for faculty members to aggressively pursue patentable ideas, any proceeds are shared with the inventor.

Iain Liggett, it turned out, was not in the habit of sharing. He intended to share the patent with no one – not his students, not his faculty colleagues, not the university. He wanted the whole stalk of bananas for himself, thank you very much. But, knowing the invention would make headlines, he had to devise a way of protecting his self-assumed claim.

His approach: the best defense is a strong offense. He by-passed the university; disclosed his invention directly to the government; used his board clout to get an early appointment with Dr. Eldon Leon, vice-president for research; and marched into the vice-president's office to tell him exactly how this particular cookie was going to crumble.

In a 40-minute meeting, the professor-trustee did his best to convince the vice-president that – because, as he claimed, only negligible, trivial details of the processes had been developed by Omnibus employees on Omnibus time in Omnibus laboratories – Omnibus University should not expect any right to any patent that might be issued.

Leon nodded his way through Liggett's spiel, but he did not buy the story. He kept his opinion to himself, though. Eldon Leon was born at night, but that night was not last night. He knew that vice-presidents serve at the pleasure of presidents, presidents at the pleasure of trustees. At the end of Liggett's monologue, without pausing, Leon said he could see no reason the professor-trustee should not proceed, and that he would informally discuss the case, as he understood it, in hypothetical terms, with the university general counsel at the next opportunity. Liggett left Leon's office encouraged and happy.

But before Liggett could exit the reception area, the vice-president had picked up his telephone and made for himself the next opportunity to discuss the case, as he understood it, in hypothetical terms, with the university general counsel, Richard Nailer. "I've just been lectured by a con man, Dick." Leon proceeded to share the trumped-up story.

"Whoo-boy! Preposterous!" Nailer whispered when Leon had finished.

"What should I do?" said Leon.

"Eldon, your mother and teachers taught you what you *should* do. But, assuming you like your job, you know there's not one blasted thing you *can* do," Nailer said, without a moment's hesitation. The attorney had had plenty of time, during Leon's litany, to remind himself that university attorneys also serve at the pleasure of trustees, and that in the last six months three other law firms – one a distinguished firm five times the size of his own – had formally bid to dislodge Nailer, Nailer & Nailer from its fiftysome-year niche as university general counsel.

The vice-president for research took counsel's advice. He did not do one blasted thing. A United States patent was issued to Iain Liggett, who promptly sold an exclusive license to use the mixing processes to a nationwide lawn-care firm for a million dollars up front and a whopping five percent equity position in the company. The product line, as expected, flourished. Liggett became wealthy in a matter of months, and soon thereafter lost interest in the affairs of the Omnibus University board of trustees.

Professor-trustee Liggett also abused his position in a side-ploy. He doubled the vodka in the governor's martinis at an informal gathering of a few trustees and state officials one evening. Then he proceeded to successfully wheedle an agreement from the state's chief executive that the departments of transportation, public works, and natural resources would use only Liggett's proprietary combination products in all of their lawn- and turf-care operations statewide.

Ever the astute businessman, professor-trustee Liggett followed up that self-serving evening the next morning by faxing a confirmatory memorandum to the governor, detailing the agreement. Whether the governor remembered having agreed to anything may never be known. But he probably did remember talking about turf-care products with someone within earshot of others. So the governor honored the agreement.

True to his selfish bent, however, Liggett saw no reason to overexert himself reciprocating the favor. ("What's in it for me?" he always wanted to know.) A few months later, he flatly told a gubernatorial administrative assistant "no" when invited to consider serving on the governor's reelection campaign committee.

Crassness (here read *dry rot*) can pay off big time in the university (here read *the ivory tower*) when officials see through naughty schemes but look the other way.

And as for the trustees, although duly sworn to do all they can in the best interests of the university, actually they provide minimal oversight. In this case, Russell, Drysdale, Humpherys, Snell-Schumacher, and several other trustees eventually heard the whole repulsive story. But in the clique's time-honored tradition – "I'll let you do your thing if you'll let me do mine" – it never came up for discussion by a group larger than two. Not even when the professor-trustee would excuse himself from the board table for a moment to visit the men's room or to use his cellular telephone.

> No weapon in the arsenals of the world is so formidable
> as the will and moral courage of free men and women.
> **Ronald W. Reagan (b. 1911)**
> **Fortieth President, United States of America**

REMEMBERING ... *The Tales of Two Students*

Whatever colleges and universities choose to spend their money on is called a cost. But colleges and universities have been greatly expanding what they do – and as long as they spend the rising tuition on something, that something will be called a cost.

Thomas Sowell

Trustees know that the institution's response to rising costs and changed circumstances cannot simply be one of raising tuition; what is required is a deeper concern with an institution's priorities and processes, and a willingness to make changes where appropriate. **Pew Higher Education Roundtable**
Policy Perspectives, **July 1995, Vol. 6 No. 2, p. 4**

Thousands of graduates are lamenting the long-term consequences of taking on debt to finance an education: a drain on their monthly income, a crimp on lifestyle and meager savings or investments. But failure to meet student loan obligations could spell financial disaster – wages can be garnished, tax refunds intercepted and credit rescinded ... . Twenty years ago, students took out about $1.20 in loans for every $1.00 in federal grants they received. Today that proportion is $3.80 in student loans for each $1.00 in grants, according to government reports ... the total median amount of educational loans taken out jumped 153 percent, to $16,417 per student in 1995 from $6,488 in 1991, raising median monthly payments to $180 from $80. Students take out an average $17,000 in loans today.

Vivian Marino, AP business writer
Tulsa World, **September 23, 1996, p. A7**

Thirty years from now the big university campuses will be relics. Universities won't survive. It's as large a change as when we first got the printed book.

Peter F. Drucker, Professor of Management
Peter F. Drucker Graduate Management Center
of the Claremont Graduate School
Interview published in *Forbes*, March 10, 1997

How can educational institutions justify raising tuition at a time when inflation has nearly disappeared and when the stock market's stunning performance has boosted college endowments about 74%, on average, in the past four years?

Tristan Mabry
The Wall Street Journal, **March 12, 1999, p. A2**

CHAPTER 3

ACADEMIC LEADERS WHO DO NOT LEAD

> An effective administrator soon learns that the greatest congestion is near the bottom of the ladder; the higher one gets on it the more rare real competence becomes. The most difficult resource to acquire is adequate human ability, particularly the kind possessed by people who continue to grow and not by those who with a little success puff up and sit still with a self-satisfied look .... I concluded that one of the secrets of success in the administration of a large organization is one's ability to surround himself with bright, able people. The more successful corporations or institutions, I noticed, always had a large reservoir of young persons being trained for higher responsibilities.
>
> **John A. Hannah (1902-1991)**
> **President, Michigan State University (1941-1969)**

The halls of academe are filled with administrators who lack leadership, skills, and vision. We know by the examples of some, however, that courageous, effective leadership is possible. It is a happy occasion when a person ascends to a leadership position whose vision and statesmanship, courage and tenacity, and ability to inspire and motivate people change the course of institutional history. Anthony Adams Ainsworth was such a person. The fates were looking over Omnibus University when the trustees named Dr. Ainsworth president about the time the university started planning for its second century of service.

As president of Omnibus for nearly three decades, Adams Ainsworth demonstrated broad vision, resolute will, and more than anything else, a capacity to achieve. He was friendly and open, humble and unselfish, of impeccable character and high integrity, pragmatic and action-oriented. Much of the credit for transforming Omnibus University from a small, backwater institution to a bustling multiversity playing on the world scene goes to Adams Ainsworth.

Ainsworth redefined Omnibus, outlining a formula for institutional excellence, garnering commitments and support both on- and off-campus. He considered Omnibus's public-service obligation as a mandated mission not merely a vehicle for soliciting public support.

President Ainsworth believed the greatest asset of public colleges and universities to be the confidence of the people. He knew, though, that the public can be fickle, that it has to be cultivated through honest service, fertilized with new ideas to meet the public's ever-changing needs, priorities, and whims.

To learn firsthand what the people needed and wanted, Adams Ainsworth traveled to every county in the state to visit with Omnibus University alumni as well as business, social, school, and church groups; service clubs; city, county, and state officials. Once he knew the people's concerns, hopes, and priorities, he proceeded to honor them.

Seeing that Omnibus would need more public monies, and having great respect for the political process, president Ainsworth got to know each member of the state legislature as well as the state's elected representatives in Washington. He believed every one of them should be treated as an important individual. After all, each had one vote.

Ainsworth also believed university executive officers should not compete with professional lobbyists in the halls of the state and federal capitols. He dealt with legislators in their home districts – in their homes, their places of work, wherever convenient. If they wanted to turn the occasion into a media opportunity, Adams Ainsworth cooperated, but he would let his host make the arrangements.

Fearing he might be perceived as an elitist and lose public support, Ainsworth was careful in his use of the word *excellence*. When he did, it was in the context of institutional excellence requiring *people* and *programs, facilities* and *funding*. Adam Ainsworth knew that merely saying Omnibus was a good university would not make it so. Neither would advertising hoopla. So he zealously worked to upgrade the four components of academic excellence to assure the quality Omnibus needed and deserved.

People. Throughout a period of huge growth, Ainsworth never lost sight of the importance of keeping in touch with the people. No institution is better than the collective abilities, ambitions, and attitudes of its faculty, staff, and students. Ainsworth repeatedly demonstrated his sincere interest in people – their needs, their aspirations.

President Ainsworth believed public-supported colleges are obligated to provide education for all people – rich, poor, man, woman, those of color, those of different cultures and origins – who could benefit from it.

> Open the doors to all ... . Let the children of the rich
> and the poor take their seats together and know of no dis-
> tinction save that of industry, good conduct, and intellect.
> **William T. Harris (1835-1909)**
> **American educator and philosopher**

Adams Ainsworth favored being soft in admitting students but hard in terms of academic-performance expectations. He sought to provide the kind of education that would help graduates live meaningful lives and fulfill their potential to contribute to society. Lack of funds was not a reason to reject the poor and admit the wealthy. To those who recommended that inevitable budgetary shortfalls be addressed by increasing tuition and fees, Adams Ainsworth's reply was that to turn away students because they could not afford the cost would create an elite class as well as deprive society of greatly needed future leaders.

Anthony Adams Ainsworth liked students, and they reciprocated. This interaction brought about changes in campus mores, student services, and governance. To give students an opportunity to participate in decision-making, president Ainsworth routinely held open forums with students.

At one meeting, students complained that the course-registration rigmarole had turned into a fiasco. The president assured them he would look into the matter. And he did. The next registration period, he personally spent over an hour in each of several lines with students who eventually were turned away all-too-often with the "that-course-is-filled" message. President Ainsworth bypassed the bureaucratic capillaries, went for the jugulars, and when registration time rolled around the next semester, registration by computer or by telephone was in force.

When faculty members left Omnibus for whatever reasons, President Ainsworth advocated replacing them with the best people available. He knew the quickest way to improve a unit was to recruit personnel who were academically stronger than those being replaced. He also knew that, if the faculty had veto privileges, it would vote for people no better than themselves, and he operated accordingly.

> A bureaucracy which recognizes everybody equally and rewards them equally, sooner or later lowers itself to its least common denominator.
> **John A. Hannah (1902-1991)**
> **President, Michigan State University (1941-1969)**

No university can consistently recruit and retain a faculty of excellence without an outstanding library and the high-quality classrooms, laboratories, and support facilities that undergird distinguished teaching, scholarly research, and timely public service.

> The library is the university – its most valued resource,
> its most precious and significant imperative.
>
> **John, Lord Russell (1792-1878)**
> **British statesman**

Programs. The Ainsworth Years at Omnibus evolved from thorough knowledge of what the institution was and a rational vision of what it should become.

Adams Ainsworth insisted on honoring and protecting the rights of faculty members to inquire, speak, teach, and write in their academic discipline, subject only to peer professional judgment. He rebuffed outside censors and resisted his own temptations to ask faculty members to be more discreet. But he frequently and openly disagreed with those who resisted programmatic changes. He was contemptuous of faculty who were reluctant to make changes they thought might disrupt their academic routine and disciplinary turf.

> It is the responsibility of the board of trustees to protect
> the public interest. The public interest and the selfish interest
> of the employees of the university are not always the same –
> in fact, I think in most instances they are not the same.
>
> **John A. Hannah (1902-1991)**
> **President, Michigan State University (1941-1969)**

Facilities and Funding. Anthony Adams Ainsworth courageously risked criticism and occasional failure as he moved aggressively on numerous fronts. A ninefold increase in enrollment during The Ainsworth Years, a broadening of curricula, new research efforts, and programs providing needed services created demand for additional residence halls, classroom and research facilities, offices, and other support facilities. Ainsworth effectively used the doubling of student enrollment in one four-year period to impress upon legislators the need to appropriate more monies. The residence halls were constructed with nonappropriated, self-liquidating bond monies, and many new programs initially were funded by aggressive private fundraising efforts, including precedent-setting grants from several foundations.

President Ainsworth kept the university administration lean, but hired key people who were able to convene faculty and staff members who did not agree on much of anything, to start and keep asking questions, and listen to and heed the answers. Over a few hours, days, or weeks, the change-resistant persons usually would themselves change, becoming full participants in resolving the problem of the moment. That is not to say that Ainsworth surrounded himself with yes-people. Quite the contrary. He listened attentively to his critics, his detractors, to those who held views differing from his. If they were right, he himself changed.

> Compliments are nice to receive but they don't really help us to improve.
>
> **John A. Hannah (1902-1991)**
> **President, Michigan State University (1941-1969)**

President Ainsworth believed it is crucial to have effective vertical and horizontal communication; that all faculty and staff need to know what is going on and that they should not have to learn about it by reading the local newspaper. His effective people skills facilitated Ainsworth's goal of mobilizing faculty and staff, students and parents, alumni and friends, people around the state and around the world to join hands and hearts in making Omnibus a renowned university.

♋ ♋ ♋

If president Anthony Adams Ainsworth were alive today, he would not be amused by some of the shenanigans going on in higher education, even at his beloved Omnibus University. As one example, mounting pressure for colleges and universities to be more accountable for their use of public monies has focused on *academic assessment* – determining particularly how much learning occurs between a student's matriculation and graduation. The accrediting body overseeing Omnibus required that every institution in its region initiate in-house academic assessment. Rather than simply imposing another unfunded mandate, the association recommended that the schools charge students a special fee of up to $1 per credit hour. For Omnibus, with over 30,000 full-time students, at $1 per hour, revenue would total approximately $1 million annually.

Special fees have become a way for bureaucratic administrators who embrace *status quo* – who avoid seriously considering cutting expenses, avoid using technology to increase effectiveness of student services, avoid rightsizing administrative staff – to impose additional taxes on trusting students, most of whom are struggling to make financial ends meet.

At Omnibus University, the usual process of imposing new special fees for art classes, field trips, laboratory courses, and the like is to present a proposal for board approval. In this case, though, administrators okayed collecting the fee even before they knew how the revenue would be spent. No cost estimate for administering the program was available, so it was easy to decide to impose the maximum recommended fee.

President Fred Finnigan appointed an *ad hoc* committee of faculty and staff members and charged them to plan and implement an academic-assessment program. Because of potential conflict of interest, the administration promised to keep hands-off. And with the cat away, did the mice ever play!

First, a faculty member was tapped as program director and given overall control. Less than one full-time staffer was needed to do the clerical tasks, but three were employed. Two of them – special friends of a key campus administrator – were simultaneously enrolled in the university, earning their bachelor's degrees. Turning sleazy right away, the committee members decided to pay themselves each two months' summer salary for committee service, an all-time first. Faculty members commonly devote time serving on committees and councils for the common good with no special remuneration.

The committee also earmarked special-fee money to fund pilot research projects they themselves would conduct. And they paid their own expenses to attend national meetings to report the results, lengthening their professional resumes in the process. Privately, committee members referred – with grins, jiggles, nudges, throat-clearing, and winks – to the special-fee revenue as their private slush fund. All paid by levies on trusting, uninformed students.

A new dimension of the issue came to the campus administration's attention when the program director left Omnibus, necessitating an interim audit. It turned up major surprises. One dean, who all along had complained about how the special-fee funds were being used, offered to try to straighten out the situation. That proved to be a difficult task. When the president described the ugly lay of the land to naive vice-presidents, deans, and directors, there were no gasps or sighs. Zero! Most reacted by scheming about how they could arrange to have a share of the largesse directed into their own money pots. Each had a pet project that – from their respective, selfish perspectives – "needed" to be funded by the excess revenue being generated by the special fee.

The administrators could have either considered the special-fee revenue as support only for its authorized, expressed, intended purpose or else reduced this unfair tax. They chose neither route. To the person, the scheming administrators – all professed friends of students – considered the money up for grabs. In the ensuing tussle – a hybrid between a debate in the well of the House of Representatives and a World Championship Wrestling match – several campus units desperately tried to gain unilateral control of the academic-assessment program's purse. And president Finnigan stood by, watching but not intervening to restore ethical integrity and order because he was too busy scrambling to secure *his* share.

Only cursory thought has ever been given to reducing the special fee being levied on unsuspecting students. True to tradition in the ivory tower, students are being bilked in just one more pecuniary rape, and milking this boondoggle-turned-cash-cow is not likely to end soon.

$$\mathcal{S} \; \mathcal{S} \; \mathcal{S}$$

President Ainsworth would not have tolerated such a mess. But many of today's administrators differ from Ainsworth and his ilk. Each has unique flaws, but these sustainers of *status quo* have in common one characteristic: an inability to lead. This defect comes in different flavors and colors and sizes, but it is the common denominator. The root cause in most cases: these people lack respect for any constituency other than themselves. Virtually to the person, they are shameless egocentrists.

At a large university, there may be as many as a dozen or more academic units administered by just as many deans. Maybe only one or two are certifiable weaklings. But an institution's council of deans is like the proverbial chain: the weakest ones set the tone. Why? Because of a tacit conspiracy of silence. Because of a seemingly mortal fear of catastrophe if one were simply honest, said what was obvious to all, and then went on to rectify the situation. But this silence – part of the cover-your-arse syndrome so evident among people who would rather keep their positions than do what they agreed to do when they assumed them – results in everyone pussyfooting through the graveyard at night whistling to himself.

📀 📀 📀

Some administrators grow while serving in positions of responsibility. Others merely swell.
Adlai E. Stevenson (1900-1965)
American politician

On a split vote, Dr. Urbane Tripp was appointed dean of Omnibus's College of Business, a position he held onto for almost two decades. It soon became obvious to all that Dean Tripp was a pompous photo-op-seeker who would go to any length to please university-level administrators, commonly at the expense of the best interests of the college he nominally led. Tripp went so far as to purchase a house on the same block as that of the provost to whom he reported, so he and his social-climbing spouse became chummy with the provost's family, quickly learning the likes and dislikes of that key member of his survival team.

The Urb Tripps joined the provost's country club, civic club, and church; patronized the same bank and supermarket; volunteered for the same community projects – all enabling them to walk and work alongside their boss and his spouse. They also attended the same movies, plays, and symphony performances; visited the same museums and galleries. The women shopped together. Their extended families even took vacation cruises together.

As dean of business, Urb Tripp had ready access to leaders of businesses and industries all over the state. Through them he arranged for himself *and* his provost lucrative board appointments, consultantships, and favors, and arranged travel abroad to visit Omnibus projects in developing countries. Their spouses especially enjoyed those trips – shopping, touring, gifts.

This key link in assuring career survival was nailed down even tighter when Tripp learned from experience of the favor he could engender with university administrators by exercising extreme frugality in managing the college's financial resources. Then, when the higher administration needed a few hundred thousand dollars for some pet project or to balance the university budget, they could count on Urb Tripp to come to the rescue by returning business college monies to the university treasury.

As a result, for example, he made no attempt to retain faculty members when Omnibus was being raided by top institutions and corporations. His philosophy was that it was a distinct privilege to work at Omnibus, and if someone elected to graze in perceived greener pastures, he told department heads to let them go, that they could be replaced by any of several on a ready list of prospects, that this would result in "salary savings".

The strategy worked. Upper administrators remembered Tripp's cooperative attitude when a disgruntled college faculty marched into the provost's office asking for a comprehensive review of their dean's performance. No such review happened.

The years rolled by, and so did missed opportunities for college leadership. As other colleges at Omnibus added major programs and facilities, the College of Business faculty questioned their plight and became restless. Finally, discontent with dean Tripp's bungling and time-buying tactics reached the point where faculty members joined hands and hearts in discussions of how they might best go about getting fresh, vibrant leadership.

The waves of heightened concern became more frequent and noisy. But every time Urb Tripp learned about behind-the-scenes discussion of his ineptness, he would methodically identify the leaders of discontent and call them to his office, one-at-a-time. There, always making it a point to have his suit coat on, he would apply the prestige of a trip down the hall for a cup of coffee with the dean. During these tête-à-têtes, he would offer travel perquisites, items of research equipment, key committee appointments, and other goodies, such as the promise of a special salary bonus the next time around. Invariably, he managed to buy more time.

Many conscientious professors would get torqued-up for a while, hopeful that new leadership soon would be on its way. But then, seeing the turn of events and watching faculty colleagues succumbing to the dean's charm and pressure, once again they would give up, and another wave would pass. After all, one can sustain a high level of anxiety, discontent, and torque only so long. If no changes are forthcoming, no sign of progress to be seen, there is a tendency to back off, and to move ahead with one's more immediate professional opportunities and responsibilities. Dean Tripp well-recognized this trait of human behavior, and used it in his calculating and manipulating. "They've shot their wads, so now they'll have to stop and reload," he would tell confidantes.

How does a faculty stuck with a professional survivor for dean – an inept leader, viewed by faculty as not being good enough to keep, and by university administrators as a cooperator worth keeping – persuade a higher administration that they need and deserve better leadership?

If the faculty is fortunate, an opportunity will come along for such a dean to move to a foundation, a governmental appointment, or a business position that takes the professional time-buyer off their hands. This enables those in higher administration – persons who commonly avoid confrontation and who are themselves often professional time-buyers and decision-avoiders – to get off the hook still intact. Of course, in such cases, while the academy gains from the leave-taking, some other sector of society loses.

Faculty and staff seeking new leadership should neither overestimate their own ability to give a professional time-buyer the proverbial gate nor underestimate the ability of a pompous, deep-rooted survivor to finesse the workings of the ivory tower.

> A life spent in making mistakes is not only more honorable but more useful than a life spent in doing nothing.
> **George Bernard Shaw (1856-1950)**
> **Irish-born British author**

ℬ ℬ ℬ

Sarah Emma Kline grew up in a community of God-fearing, nonargumentative, unpretentious people. By the time she reached college, Sarah was a self-assured young woman of average intellect. Her self-righteous self-image fed an extreme ambition, but in reality she was destined to confirm The Peter Principle.

Although Dr. Sarah Emma Kline quickly found a place as an assistant professor of history at a mid-sized university, her thesis in the history of science bounced around scholarly journals for years, but never passed peer review for publication. Six years into her career, her professional activities dossier was thin. She was promoted to associate-professor rank and tenured mainly because her dean reminded the university promotion and tenure committee to remember the realities of affirmative action. In another era, Kline probably would not have been retained. Although she exuded a special presence when she strode into a room, she was confirming "The Principle" already as an assistant professor. The winds of the times gave her a second chance, and she knew it.

Before long, Sal Kline was leaning toward a career in administration. Her research program never gained wings, and she simply did not enjoy teaching. Yet her healthy self-confidence and her family's continuous reassurances convinced her she had much to offer academe. She announced her availability for all manner of boards and committees – department, college, university, professional association, Sunday school, United Way, township water authority, you name it. She would cancel lectures to attend a workshop for administrator wannabes anywhere in the country. When her university travel funds ran out, she would pay her own way, intent upon gaining evidence of quasi-administrative experience to pad her curriculum vitae.

Through it all, Kline stayed true to certain childhood Sunday school lessons that really stuck with her: avoid conflict; "the meek shall inherit the earth"; and so on. She ran from confrontations, but that does not mean she was indecisive. Her decision-making took place under the table, behind the screen, in the dark of night. Some committees she chaired never met, but still managed to submit final reports. Sarah Kline simply would draft the report, ship it out to committee members, then walk around to their individual offices to meet with them, agreeing to make their perfunctory modifications, getting their signatures. Of course, in all this, the benefits of committee debate were lost.

Sarah Kline's overall tack played right into a recent trend in the academy: the rise of lackluster, unprovocative administrators. She played her cards right – close to her chest – and took the first minor administrative post at a minor institution that she was offered. She performed in predictable style, and earned a reputation as a do-nothing director, routinely winning the booby prize at administrators parties as being "the one in our midst least likely to make a mistake". Only Kline herself did not know the prize was especially designed for her, and not intended to be a compliment.

All the while, Sal Kline kept several lines in the job-search water, even though she was already a step or two beyond confirming "The Principle". As will happen, particularly nowadays, the dullard Kline landed the arts and sciences deanship at a name institution: Omnibus University. The college had been without a permanent dean for two years, prompting the provost to assume control and engage in a "directed search". Trustee Malcomb Russell himself proclaimed, "I am just simply convinced Sarah'll be just the ticket." And that, as we know, was that.

In less than a month, everyone up and down the line who cared enough to find out had discovered that Sarah Kline was a misfit in her new role. Over her head in intellect, vision, people skills. Malcomb Russell reserved judgment for a year or better, but eventually even he admitted that dean Kline was "a problem".

Sheer incompetence is one thing. But Sarah Kline compounded her case. As soon as she realized she was in danger of drowning, she grabbed for her favorite straw: a candy-striped number comprising in the stripes a penchant for super-delegation to those who answered to her on a background of self-righteous, self-confident self-esteem well on its way to becoming a disgusting brand of egocentrism.

Of course, Sarah Kline was Omnibus's problem. The word was out from coast to coast. Finally, *everybody* knew she had confirmed "The Principle". Unfortunately, the period between general recognition and successful resolution in such cases can be excruciatingly long. In Kline's case, eight years. Eight years in which the arts and sciences at Omnibus flopped and floundered; morale across the board hit an all-time low; and the legislature's joint committee on education two years in a row temporarily held up Omnibus's allocation of state funds to emphasize its point: replace dean Kline.

As for Sal Kline herself, she was ever upbeat, apparently oblivious to the crises always swirling around and through the college. Actually, she was directly responsible for the demise of that college. Although she was incompetent, intellectually and otherwise, to fulfill her job description, she apparently never admitted this to herself. But she must have known, which may explain why she became a super-delegator.

Kline delegated *full responsibility* for operating the college's departments to their heads. But she reserved *full authority* for herself, regularly entertaining faculty complaints without informing the heads, and meddling and overruling the heads even on trivial decisions. When a head would make a request of dean Kline, a decision – or no decision – nine times out of ten was rendered without the head ever having the opportunity to further discuss the matter with her. Despite repeated requests, some heads went more than a year without having a one-on-one meeting with dean Sarah Kline. That is, except the stilted once-a-year performance evaluation, which usually lasted fifteen or twenty minutes and often touched on neither the head's performance nor the dean's evaluation of it.

In one infamous stretch, Kline canceled fifteen of twenty-four monthly meetings with department heads, a couple of them three months in advance. The tone of those meetings sometimes became contentious, found the dean in a vulnerable posture, put her on the spot.

As for the associate deans, dean Kline had confirmed another principle: first-class deans appoint first-class associates, second-classers appoint third-classers. The associate deans all knew that professional lives were being destroyed willy nilly, that the college's programs were on a fast slope to netherworld. Their only honorable courses would have been either to raise Cain, trying to force the dean to change her ways, or end their association with her. The associate deans not only raised no Cain and submitted no letters of resignation, they also unabashedly went on accepting hefty checks every payday.

When her superiors raised questions about matters gone sour – just as she did when faculty members, department heads, and external advisory committees got cranky – dean Sarah Kline would reach for the trap-door tripper, identify a scapegoat and eliminate yet another department head to whom she had delegated all responsibility but no authority. When matters got dicey, she simply blamed the delegatees and eliminated them, one by one. By the time external pressures from legislators and advisory committees and internal pressures from department heads and faculty reached the breaking point, dean Sarah Kline had, in eight years, delegated all responsibility but no authority to twenty-seven heads of ten departments. Still her stubbornness – all based on self-conscious, self-righteous self-esteem – carried the day, day after day after day. "The lady can't take a hint," is how one professor put it.

President Fred Finnigan and provost Charles Stendahl had known for years that dean Kline was a problem. And then there was her unmitigatedly negative five-year evaluation report. But for reasons of their own – namely, they wanted to keep the College of Arts and Sciences weak and vulnerable so they could plunder its moneybags – they had deferred the action they had privately agreed would have to come sooner or later. Finally, the pressures became so great they simply had to act. When the tried-and-true external-internal pincer was applied, they had no choice. So dean Sarah Kline was "asked to resign". Conservative estimates have it that the legacy of Sal Kline in arts and sciences will take twenty-years-plus to turn around, if ever.

ॐ ॐ ॐ

Nicholas Woolfre grew up in a family of privilege á la the 1950s. An only child, Nicholas's father practiced law, his mother medicine. But he spent more time with his governess and the maid and the houseman. These servants enjoyed their work in the Woolfre home – warm in winter, cool in summer, windows always spotless, larders always loaded – and they rightly sensed that, in order to get along, they should wait hand and foot on the little-man-of-the-house.

Nicholas Woolfre attended a preparatory school – as a townie, still living at home – that tried to instill well-rounded character in its charges, but never expected them to raise a finger. The school's cooks and waiters, maids and gardeners, boatsmen and hostelers did that. And of course the servants were still on staff at home. Nick Woolfre expected that kind of service the rest of his life. He grew up to be an aloof, lazy man.

For one with his roots, Woolfre had a career goal many would consider weird. He wanted to become a classics scholar. So, of course, that is what he became. He earned degrees at those citadels of classics study, Harvard and Yale. His prodigious intellect was not taxed in all this, though. True to his laziness, he exerted himself only enough to top the class, no more, then spent his spare time keeping up-to-the-minute on the inside machinations of the Republican National Committee and blowing about it to everyone within earshot, interested or not.

Just because he was lazy does not mean Woolfre was unambitious. But few knew what his potential on any front really was. All through private grade and preparatory schools and nearly nine years of ivy-league college, Nick Woolfre was an oddity – a glad-handing lone wolf. Everyone knew him by name and reputation, but he was neither particularly admired nor very much liked by his fellow students. To the bones, he was an unsociable person, although he has been careful never to show this, intuitively recognizing that to do so would be impolitic. Everyone in his presence has always felt vaguely uneasy with his surface friendliness. In fact, he has respected and consulted with no one about anything. He has always kept his own supremely confident counsel.

Woolfre easily gained an assistant professorship at another ivy-league school, starting the week after defending his doctoral dissertation on humane concepts of the French Classical movement. His career enjoyed a steady up-trend for the first ten years. He did what he wanted to do, and no more. His brainpower was directed partly at working the system so others would do the real work while he remained above that fray, as truly befitted a person of his place, standing, and upbringing.

But then, in Nicholas Woolfre's year eleven, the humanities dean tapped to head the classics department a no-nonsense fellow who had grown up in a steel-mill town and went on with his own brand of brains and energy to gain an education and build a career as a classics professor at a midwestern land-grant university. Woolfre had thought it was beneath his dignity to engage in the process of identifying the next department head.

He had arrived at every candidate's interview luncheon late, left early, and skipped every interview seminar.

The new man was a straight-talker. In their first meeting after he arrived to head the department, he told Nick Woolfre he had big plans for putting Nick's brains and oratory skills to better use. In addition to everything he was already doing, Nick should also offer a service course in classical studies that would appeal to the student masses! The new head told him in no uncertain terms that he was not working anywhere near his potential, and that his future salary increases and promotion to full professor would depend upon his approaching that potential.

Nicholas Woolfre felt his gut go into an uproar, and the dyspepsia went on for months. He was horrified by what the head had said, and could not get it off his mind. He knew he was not fulfilling his potential, knew he never had, knew he never had intended to. He felt threatened, out of control of his professional destiny for the first time. He became depressed, and grabbed for his particular straw. He called his travel agent, ordered a first-class air ticket to Geneva, went to the Swiss mountain chalet he had inherited, spent a week there trying to sort matters out.

On the flight back home, Nick Woolfre's spirits were high. He had decided. He knew he had to leave his present job. His only option would be to take an administrative job. He would land at an institution beneath his dignity, but that was that.

He landed at Omnibus University, as director of the inter-college honors program. It was a haughty job, in a way, but the residential program required its director to live in the honors dormitory. Nicholas Woolfre had never before in his life spent one single night in a dormitory. Within two months – with the provost's okay – he had arranged to move to the biggest house on the Collegeville real estate market at the time. He had landed on his feet, as always.

One thing led to another, and within five years Nicholas Woolfre was tapped to become dean of the arts and sciences to follow Sarah Emma Kline. All of a sudden, he abandoned his scholarly streak. Survival became job one! He *was* indecisive, and did not think he really had to make decisions. Nicholas Woolfre, as Urbane Tripp, was a time-buyer. "Well, of course, I won't be making any changes until I've had a chance to get my feet on the ground," he would say, "to get a feel for the place, to learn what *you* want." Truth be told, as always, he listened to no one but himself.

A rudderless ship soon turns into a deteriorating ship, a rotting ship, a dry-rotting ship. Again, campus administrators saw opportunity, and raided the arts and sciences college treasury as never before. Faculty and staff reductions were huge and demoralizing. All the while, Woolfre simply quoted philosophers and politicians in the original Greek or Latin or French or German with an ironic smile on his smug face.

Nicholas Woolfre received a scathing five-year review, but talked president Fred Finnigan into letting him "hang in there" for "one more year, two max". In the meantime, he worked furiously to find his next place to jump to, and he found it. And he landed on his feet again, as always.

If you can prevaricate with a straight face, and explain away with an excuse and two ancient quotes every hickey on your record, you will be attractive to most search committees, many of which in this day and age seem to be dying to trust Pollyanna *and* the tooth fairy!

> When the situation was manageable it was neglected, and now that it is thoroughly out of hand, we apply too late the remedies which might have effected a cure. There is nothing new in the story. It is as old as the sibylline books. It falls into that long dismal catalogue of the fruitlessness of experience and the confirmed unteachability of mankind. Want of foresight, unwillingness to act when action would be simple and effective, lack of clear thinking, confusion of counsel until the emergency comes, until self-preservation strikes its jarring gong – these are the features which stimulate the endless repetition of history.
>
> **Sir Winston Churchill (1874-1965)**
> **Prime Minister, United Kingdom**
> **(1940-1945; 1951-1955)**

REMEMBERING ... *The Tales of Two Students*

What often is missing is the action on campus to carry out the ideals we so fervently profess. Although we are experts at describing how governments and corporations need to be more just or egalitarian, the academic world itself is highly concerned with rank and status, and those with power frequently overlook the many people on campus who occupy low-status positions and are struggling financially.

Sunny Merik, Editor, Santa Clara University *Spectrum*
"Helping Higher Education's Working Poor"
*The Chronicle of Higher Education***, July 26, 1996, p. B1**

Those of four-family income categories going to college in 1994 were: 58% of those with incomes up to $23,000; 68% of those with incomes of $23,000-$41,000; 77% of those in the $41,000 to $68,000 category; and 88% of those with incomes above $68,000.

"Shaping the Future"
Journal of Postsecondary-Education Opportunity
The California Higher Education Policy Center, April 1997

Reacting to growing costs, Congress through the '80s and '90s expanded the student loan program, while scrimping on no-strings-attached grants. Undergraduates can now borrow up to $46,000 and graduate students $138,500 in federally guaranteed loans – and many approach these high limits. So far this decade, students have borrowed at least $140 billion – more than the total student borrowing over the past three decades combined. Since 1977, median student loan debt has leapt from $2000 to about $15,000.

Joshua Wolf Shenk
*US News & World Report***, June 9, 1997, p. 38**

The preponderance of complaints about higher education focuses on the rising cost of a college education. Policymakers wonder if perhaps institutions of higher education are being run inefficiently. For the increase in cost, where is the increase in quality?

Philip S. Moore, Director of Assessment
University of South Carolina, "Assessing Performance-Based
Funding," Adult Assessment Forum, Fall 1997

CHAPTER 4

PROFESSORS WHO DO NOT PUBLISH AND DO NOT PERISH

> They defend their errors as if they were defending their inheritance.
>
> **Edmund Burke (1729-1797)**
> **British statesman and orator**

Dewey Ertle's parents operated a fruit orchard in the Pacific Northwest – apples, pears, and bing cherries. Young Dewey, too young to serve in the armed forces during World War II, did his part to make Ertle Orchard a profitable enterprise.

Fruit farming magazines were stacked together with the Portland *Oregonian*, *Time*, and *National Geographic* in the Ertle living room, current fruit-production handbooks shelved alongside the *Reader's Digest* condensed books and *World Book* encyclopedias. For Dewey the teenager, tree-fruit farming came second nature. He read everything about it he could get his hands on, especially any popular news of research and technology.

So when time for college rolled around, it was natural for Dewey Ertle to focus on a career in either the fruit industry or horticultural science. On his first day at the state land-grant agri-culture college, he met with the professor who was to be his aca-demic adviser, Dr. Quentin Forbes, a plant pathologist in horti-culture research. Forbes, in his mid-thirties at the time, already enjoyed an international reputation. Dewey had read about his research on insect pests of pear trees. That first meeting went so well that, on the spot, Dr. Forbes offered Dewey Ertle a part-time job in his laboratory.

The wages would not be the main benefit of that job, though. The professor was so impressed by the young man's curiosity, gumption, and knowledge that, by mid-October, Forbes was advising Dewey to enroll in courses that would prepare him for graduate school and a research career.

After graduation, Dewey Ertle did pursue graduate studies in California. He was in his fourth semester, making exceptional progress, when the head of horticultural sciences at Omnibus University cold-called him one afternoon. "We're going to do whatever it takes to convince you to leave your studies out West and come join us right now, here at Omnibus," Professor Ragsdale said. "We have big plans, and they include you, Dewey Ertle! We know more about you than your mother knows! This college is committed to a brand-new program in pomological physiology, and we want you at the helm."

Ertle was flattered but flabbergasted. After discussing both pluses and downsides with his major adviser, he decided to leave his studies in California and join Omnibus – hundreds of miles away.

At Omnibus, Dewey Ertle – fresh master of science diploma in his hip pocket – threw every bit of his considerable intellect, energy, and enthusiasm into establishing what soon would be called the Fruit Physiology Research Center (FPRC), a semi-autonomous operation that became the world's fountain-head for pomological physiology.

Along the way, he earned a Ph.D. degree. His doctoral-study advisory committee was chaired by Professor Ragsdale, but Dewey Ertle came as close to serving as his own director of dissertation research as could be.

From day one, Ertle was working on several fronts concurrently, putting in 60- and 70-hour weeks that would be his routine for four decades. He knew how critical financial support was going to be, and instinctively appreciated the public-service obligations of state-affiliated universities. So he built sturdy relationships with leaders of producer and processor associations in all sectors of state and regional agriculture.

Within five years, Dr. Dewey Ertle had rounded up enough contributions from the industry to construct a modern research building and orchard where scientific investigations and graduate education could flourish. An advisory board to the FPRC, comprised of tree-fruit producers and processors, met with the FPRC staff and Omnibus administrators twice a year to hear what was going on and being planned, and to offer suggestions.

Dr. Ertle did not neglect Omnibus students, either. He was an outstanding lecturer and effective teacher who made breaking news in the scientific literature live for students whose interests ranged from basic research on plant physiology to running the family fruit farm after leaving school.

For 35 years, Dr. Ertle and his colleagues – professors, students, and technicians – relentlessly pursued fundamental knowledge of physiological mechanisms in fruit trees as well as its application in the tree-fruit industry. As a group, over the years, the Omnibus team made contributions and discoveries in diverse areas, publishing over 300 scientific papers and garnering numerous awards and prizes in the process. In his twenty-sixth year at Omnibus, Dr. Ertle was named a member of the prestigious National Academy of Science. In his thirty-first year, he traveled to Israel to accept the Wolf Prize, which is, for agricultural science, the equivalent of the Nobel Prize.

ॐ ॐ ॐ

Unfortunately, the ivory tower is inhabited by its share of hapless professors, too. The career of Athens Jones – in fact his whole life – was following a traditional path. He performed well in school, earned a Ph.D. degree in ichthyology, won a tenure-track faculty position at Omnibus University from a pool of over 40 applicants, married, fathered five children. His spouse assumed the role of full-time homemaker. Family life, from all appearances, was good.

Professionally, Athens Jones seamlessly advanced through the ranks to full professor, and eventually headed a large research group in aquatic biology. By the mid-1980s, over a dozen graduate students and technicians were being supported by external grants to his research program.

Then, right about the time he reached "the big five-oh", something in Athens Jones snapped. Call it mid-life crisis, career burnout, whatever. Athens Jones did 180-degree turnabouts on all fronts.

He left his spouse of over 25 years, and moved in with a female graduate student. He grew a beard, stopped seeing his barber, and donned earrings. His sartorial taste turned to Nehru jackets, dashikis, and beads – necklaces, bracelets, and anklets. He explored the mysteries and wonders of marijuana and other recreational drugs. The lifestyle of professor Timothy Leary offered few experiences not tried by professor Athens Jones.

Athens Jones's professional productivity went to zilch. His grants came to their ends, and with them his teams of technicians and students. Also, the behavior of professor Jones, the teacher, soon became a problem. He was so unfocused in his lectures that students majoring in biology began complaining to their advisers. He was removed from courses taken by biology majors, and assigned to teach a couple of lower-level service courses. Still, a steady run of complaints came in from students and parents about his rude talk and crude jokes as well as his general appearance and demeanor in the classroom.

Eventually, Athens Jones moved into a cheap, poorly maintained apartment. When plumbing problems arose, he could not get the landlord to make necessary repairs. Being flexible to the point of eccentricity by then, he supplemented his own less-than-adequate digs with the biology department's classrooms and laboratories.

The basement of the biology building had showers and lockers for faculty and students returning from work in the field. Used sporadically, they presented a solution to Athens's predicament. When the shower at home was on the fritz, he simply would locker his belongings and take a calming, slow, warm shower in the biology building.

One morning, when he was ready to dry off and re-dress and go present a lecture, to save his life, he could not remember the combination to the padlock on his locker. There he stood in the biology building basement, dripping wet and naked as the proverbial jay bird. He cowered in the locker room till he heard voices of male students through the hallway door. On his hands and knees, yelling through the louver in the door, he begged them to ask the departmental secretary to call the physical plant. By the time the carpenters arrived with a bolt-cutter and destroyed the padlock, the class period was over. Also by that time, everyone on that end of campus was aware of Athens Jones's latest predicament.

While some of professor Jones's antics provided the campus community comic relief, there was a more serious side to his bizarre behavior. During the last three years prior to his early retirement, undergraduate students who had the misfortune of drawing him as instructor were short-changed in their educational experiences by his unseemly behavior and poor teaching.

ℐ ℐ ℐ

The Public Information Office at Omnibus University churns out a steady supply of snappy news releases, replete with flashy photographs, featuring the scholarly activities of faculty.

Some professors who seem to be productive, however, are rarely if ever featured. In most cases this is because the grapevine consensus on the work of these people is out. Their scholarship is considered to be of such poor quality that, although it runs on and on year after year, it is ignored by virtually everybody in the academy.

Take, for example, Dr. Chloe Benedict, associate professor of physical education at Omnibus. With national interest and opportunity in fitness training increasing, the university recruited Benedict about ten years ago. She immediately established connections with the manufacturers of fitness-training equipment nationwide, and soon was hosting representatives of these firms on site visits to Omnibus University. Within a few months, the flow of money supporting Benedict's research on the effectiveness of specific commercial models of exercise equipment – cycles, walking machines, stationary stairs, and so on – started, and it continues to this day.

The prevailing opinion of her peers about the quality of Chloe Benedict's scholarship is based on roughly equal parts of jealousy, snobbery, and science. *Jealousy* because Dr. Benedict's laboratory receives more external contract and grant support than any other three programs in the College of Applied Human Studies combined. *Snobbery* because many of her colleagues consider the sort of studies Benedict conducts to be *product-testing* – development at best, certainly not research. Even though *applied* is part of the college name, many of its professors are ashamed of this, preferring to view themselves (via delusions of grandeur) as basic scientists. *Science* because, at her departmental seminars and graduate students' thesis-defense meetings, it becomes clear that Benedict employs research methodology and instruments she does not understand and glibly refers to scientific literature with which she is not conversant.

One emeritus colleague has observed, "I don't care what questions Chloe chooses to pursue. There's a whole lot more difference between *good* science and *poor* science, in the first place, than between *basic* and *applied*. But Chloe's science isn't up to snuff. That's her problem."

In rationalizing her place on the Omnibus faculty, of course, professor Chloe Benedict herself chalks up her unpopularity among faculty peers to the jealousy and snobbery pieces.

A few years back, the faculty promotion-and-tenure committees of both department and college voted to deny Dr. Chloe Benedict promotion to associate-professor rank with tenure. For one thing, her list of publications is short – only four papers on work done at Omnibus. Of course, her approach is such that most of her results are proprietary and reported to the sponsoring firms, not published in peer-reviewed journals. In any case, the committees' advice was not followed. Department, college, and university administrators – excited by her laboratory's cash flow, regardless of whether her work was sound enough to be useful to anyone but an advertising agency – overruled the committees and promoted and tenured Chloe Benedict anyway.

ℐ ℐ ℐ

There was a happier time a few decades ago when universities were giddily expanding faculties to keep up with fantastic growth in student enrollments. Some faculty search and selection committees seem to have been so harried and hurried that they were not careful. Dr. Skip Firkens was hired by Omnibus University during that period. Faculty members in the Meteorology and Climatology Department knew before they hired Firkens that he would not be a faculty star. But after all, even in those halcyon days, a given faculty could accommodate only so many stars.

Unfortunately, not only has Dr. Skip (he asks to be called by all either Dr. Skip or The Skipper) turned out to be a dud; he has firmly established himself as a doltish, uncouth jerk. Dr. Skip prospered just enough to gain tenure, but even then only because his cause was advocated by gadfly faculty fans who were intent upon protecting what they believed to be the rights and entitlements of eccentric professors.

Eccentricity is one thing, incompetence another. And at promotion-and-tenure time, when the line between the two is blurred in the ivory tower, the institution typically has a problem on its hands, often for three more decades. The incompetents' scholarly productivity usually is so nearly nil that it makes no difference, and eventually their teaching assignments have to be decreased to nil, too, in deference to respect for tax- and tuition-paying students and their parents. Multiply this three-decade number by even, say, ten percent of the faculty, and at a place like Omnibus you are talking about 150 freeloaders on the professorial payroll – counting benefits, a $15-million-a-year sucking sound emanating from institutional coffers.

Dr. Skip, in particular, is the antithesis of a self-starter. Neither is he an eager or even willing collaborator or cooperator. Rarely in his office before noon, and always gone by three, some days he never shows up at all. He certainly never shows up on Tuesdays or Fridays during growing season – May through November – when he operates his booth at the farmers' market downtown from seven till six. But when asked to do something for the good of his academic unit, he almost always refuses, citing time constraints or questioning why one or another of his colleagues is not being asked to serve.

Fifteen years ago, Dr. Tina Ramirez, an adventurous and courageous department head, goaded and prodded until provost Charles Stendahl authorized her to initiate termination proceedings – provided for in the state's tenure statute – against The Skipper. But she soon wished she had not. Dr. Skip's ne'er-do-well-attorney brother-in-law blew so much smoke and threw so much muck on the preliminary process that the university's gentlemanly, image-conscious legal counsel advised that the action itself be terminated, which it was.

From that point on, Dr. Skip has been emboldened to become ever more assertive and open in his disrespect for academe, although continuing to reap the benefits of its protection and providence. He sends a steady flow of letters – offering opinions on any and every topic that comes to his fertile mind – to the editor of the *Collegeville Daily Citizen*. He also bothers himself to attend every public meeting of the faculty – department, college, university – and finds a reason to take the floor at least once every meeting to bait the parliamentarian, jeer an administrator, or taunt a fellow professor. Recently, he has taken to treating those on his electronic-mail directory to a nondescript barrage of critiques and opinions and suggestions, mostly originating from his home computer.

Hiring, promoting, and tenuring processes in colleges and universities tend to be taken more seriously nowadays than they were some years ago. But universities still have to deal daily with important, long-lasting ramifications of that laxer period. And they seem to be helpless in dealing with the cases that turn out to be most counterproductive and costly.

$$\mathscr{A} \quad \mathscr{A} \quad \mathscr{A}$$

Dr. Adam Adler was proud to be a faculty member at Omnibus University. He immensely enjoyed teaching, research, and public service; found pleasure in the collegiality of the strong Psychology Department; liked students, and they liked him. His outstanding efforts were rewarded with early promotions and prestigious national awards, large annual and special-merit salary increases, coveted appointments to journal editorial boards, book publishing opportunities, the presidency of his primary professional society, invitations to lecture extensively around the world, opportunities to consult far and wide.

For years, Adam Adler was in the fast lane. But he wanted more, especially more income. When he asked his tax accountant how he could enhance his income, Adler learned the quickest way would be to step-up his consulting activities. With his reputation and contacts, this would not be difficult, he knew.

The Omnibus policy on external consulting is typical of many institutions of higher education – one day a week, provided class meetings are covered. So Adam Adler rented an office downtown, established a consulting practice in psychometrics, and mailed information about his new venture to prospective clients near and far. His fee: $250 per hour.

Adam Adler's consulting business grew rapidly. Response exceeded his wildest dreams. Soon he was personally paying an aspiring assistant professor in the department $100 an hour to teach the class periods he had to miss. Of course, the young colleague welcomed the chance to supplement her university income.

When professor Adler's students came to his university office for advising, they would read the note on his door: "Students and Advisees: Either visit Dr. Adler at his off-campus office or see Dr. Susan Sternberg, two doors down the hall." Adler had agreed to pay Sternberg $35 for each student-advising session that resulted from this arrangement.

Adler soon began to cut himself loose from *pro bono* professional involvements, to shift time away from low-paying activities, such as guest-lecturing at other universities. He reduced the number of graduate students he mentored, and eventually phased-out his external research grants and contracts activity altogether. Knowing these decisions would not be appreciated by his department head, Adam Adler asked him to arrange a meeting with Hugo Sherbane, head of the university's foundation. He curried favor with both of these administrators by proposing to share the income of his successful private practice with various entities at Omnibus.

One account was to provide discretionary dollars for the department head to cover expenses that could not be paid with publicly appropriated monies. Others were to support programs of art, drama, music, library, and emergency loans for undergraduates. The department head and foundation director were pleasantly surprised by the size of the total package – all tax-deductible, Adler's tax adviser assured him – and they endorsed the plan before the meeting ended.

As months turned into years, Adam Adler's practice continued to prosper. He added a second associate, then a third. Importantly, he maintained his tenured full professorship with Omnibus's high-profile psychology department. It accorded him professional legitimacy, health insurance, access to inexpensive student help and the university library, a good retirement-benefits package, and many other perquisites useful to his private endeavors.

The professors should be of the most eminent in their fields, and their connections with the institution should be so fixed and stable as to enable them to carry through their ideas and labor.

Jonathan Baldwin Turner (1805-1899)
Pioneer advocate of the land-grant
college and university system

We are born into a moral environment just as we are born into a natural environment. Just as there are basic environmental necessities, like clean air, safe food, fresh water, there are basic moral necessities. What is a society without civility, honesty, consideration, self discipline?

Christina Hoff Sommers
W. H. Brady Fellow, American Enterprise Institute
Professor of Philosophy, Clark University

REMEMBERING ... *The Tales of Two Students*

In 1980, a Pell Grant covered 38 percent of the average cost of a private four-year college. Today it covers 14 percent ... . For public colleges the figures are 82 percent (1980) and 34 percent (1995) ... . Of about $35 billion that the federal government spends each year on student aid, 70 percent goes to loans and only 30 percent to grants. While these loans help many students, they also scare away many low-income students ... . People from the lowest family incomes don't use loans to substitute for grants. These people don't view loans as vehicles to opportunity, but rather as obstacles to it. What this all adds up to is a gap between families who can afford college and families who can't.

Stephen Burd, Patrick Healy, Kit Lively, and Christopher Shea
"Low-Income Students Say Their College Options Are Limited"
The Chronicle of Higher Education, **June 14, 1996, p. A11-12**

During the 10-year period from 1984-85 to 1994-95, the average tuition and fees for an undergraduate resident student taking 30 credit hours per academic year, enrolled in Texas public colleges and universities increased from $477 to $1659 – a 248 percent increase.

The Wall Street Journal, **November 20, 1996, p. T4**
Source: Texas Higher Education Coordinating Board

While there are no studies that define the price elasticity for a college degree, every fee increase does deny entrance to some students.

C. Brice Ratchford,
President, University of Missouri (1971-1976)
Memoirs of My Years at the
University of Missouri **(1996), p. 105**

Do you realize that the cost of higher education has risen as fast as the cost of health care? And for the middle-class family, college education for their children is as much of a necessity as is medical care – without it the kids have no future.

Peter F. Drucker, Professor of Management
Peter F. Drucker Graduate Management Center
of the Claremont Graduate School
Interview published in *Forbes*, March 10, 1997

CHAPTER 5

PROFESSORS WHO TEACH ... BUT NOT MUCH

> Deadwood clings to deadwood, and whole rafts begin to gather and float in the academic ocean.
>
> **Jay Parini (b. 1948)**
> **Author, biographer, and**
> **professor at Middlebury College**

> There is very little difference in people. But that little difference makes a big difference. The little difference is attitude. The big difference is whether it is positive or negative.
>
> **W. Clement Stone (b. 1902)**
> **American businessman and civic leader**

A caring attitude and concern for the overall welfare of each student serve a teacher as powerful tools. Each student needs to feel that someone notices him or her as a special, wonderful individual. Sister Susan Fenimore, a distinguished teaching professor in the Omnibus University College of Education, has been a builder of self-esteem in students for over 35 years.

Jeff Netter was one of Sister Fenimore's students of teaching mathematics. Jeff was polite and well-kempt, happy-to-be-alive, delightfully mischievous, an eager learner. Still, Sister Fenimore noticed that Jeff Netter responded positively when she took a personal interest in him.

This special teacher would handwrite the name of each of her students at the top of a sheet of notebook paper. During the semester, she would record outstanding characteristics she saw in each person. This sheet would be clipped to the final examination booklet returned at the end of the semester. Her complimentary remarks were well-received. Some said, "Really!" Others, "This is a first!"

> The mediocre teacher tells. The good teacher explains. The superior teacher demonstrates. The great teacher inspires.
>
> **William Arthur Ward**

One August, upon returning from an overseas trip, Sister Susan Fenimore was told that Jeff's mother had called. "I haven't heard from the Netters in years!" she remarked. "I wonder how Jeff is." "Jeff died in Vietnam," her colleague responded. "The funeral is tomorrow, and his parents would like you to be there."

Sister Fenimore drove through heavy rain for several hours to pay final tribute to Jeff Netter – a student like a thousand others, who nevertheless stood out in her memory.

Upon her arrival at the church, one of Jeff's cousins went to her car. "You were Jeff's teacher." She nodded. "Jeff talked a lot about you."

Following the service, Jeff's father said he wanted to share something with Sister Fenimore. He took out his billfold. "They found this in Jeff's jacket." He pulled out a folded piece of notebook paper, and carefully opened the fragile sheet. Its edges were ragged and worn, it had been folded, unfolded, refolded, and taped. Sister Fenimore caught her breath. She knew immediately what Jeff's father was holding. "Jeff obviously treasured your thoughts," Jeff's mother said.

One contributes most in life when he spends it for
something that will outlast it.

James Bell

⍥ ⍥ ⍥

We are now at a point where it is essential that we
educate students in what no one knew yesterday, and prepare
them for what no one knows yet, but what people must know
tomorrow.

Margaret Mead (1901-1978)
American anthropologist

Regardless of how independent or rebellious a student may
seem, he expects a university to provide good counsel and direction on matters related to courses and curricula. Moreover, while
the student may not be able to precisely articulate it, she expects
college to provide an intellectual adventure as well as
preparation to find a meaningful job following graduation. For
centuries, faculties have held that curricular considerations are
strictly within the domain and purview of the faculty.

An influx of international students – a welcomed trend as
they swelled tuition and fee revenues – gave Omnibus
University reason to set a policy that students for whom English
was a second language, later transfer students, and finally all
students had to pass an English proficiency examination before
being certified for graduation. Of course, the students were
assessed a fee to take the test.

The English Department readily agreed to accept the
responsibility. The faculty realized that the considerable money
so generated would be available to administer the proficiency
examination as well as to provide remedial instruction on an as-
needed basis. After two years – during which the failure rate
approached 33 percent – consternation abounded all over
campus, as well as in families of students. The English
Department had come to be perceived as having a negative
impact on the student retention and graduation rate.

Was English feathering its own nest at the expense of students? Were that many students unable to demonstrate English proficiency? What effect would this situation have on future enrollment of international and domestic students at Omnibus? Had the English faculty forgotten that salary increases of all faculty and staff are tied to total tuition monies collected, which in turn are directly affected by enrollment?

Soon English Department faculty got the message, and the pass rate soared, coming to hover in the ninetysome-percent range. Then came the question: "Are so many so proficient that testing is unnecessary, or is the examination failing to identify students lacking English proficiency?"

At that point, the Omnibus administration questioned the faculty about the wisdom of continuing to require the test. They advanced an uncommon procedural question: "Why not save students the expense and inconvenience of sitting for an English proficiency examination?"

The difficulty of undoing something in an academic bureaucracy soon became clear. The vast amount of student fees collected had come to support several faculty and staff positions. And besides, the faculty reasoned, it sounded good to have a required English proficiency examination on the books, so long as the pass rate was high and affected neither enrollment nor graduation rate. Just as there had been broad-based faculty support to institute the requirement, there was strong faculty backing to keep the test in place.

> The railroad and coal industries change faster than higher education.
>
> **Kathryn H. Anderson**
> **Economics professor, Vanderbilt University**

✄ ✄ ✄

Omnibus University has been widely recognized as a student-oriented institution. Among other strong features, it has one of the top 50 law schools in the United States. Competition among students to earn high grades – a major prerequisite for admission to law school – is fierce. So intense, in fact, that friendships among pre-law students are sometimes stretched to the breaking point. The number of applicants outnumbers those admitted by a ratio of 7:1, so the admission committee can apply substantial selection pressure. Again, grades are a most important consideration.

Professor Roland Ryan coordinated a team-taught five-hour course in accounting, Accountancy 101. This course is required for pre-law students and recognized by the law school associate dean for academic affairs – a tough but fair individual who coordinated the work of the admission committee – as a reliable indicator of what to expect gradewise of law students.

Accountancy 101 was taught in a large, modern, classroom that was convenient to student traffic. The high demand for the course meant it filled early, and when students came to Professor Ryan with special reasons as to why they "had to have the course this semester", he would try to accommodate their needs. He would have folding chairs set up in the aisles and let students sit in the window wells and even on the floor in front of the first row of seats. The students never complained. They simply wanted to enroll in the course when they wanted to enroll.

The policies of this team-taught course were determined by faculty consensus. For one thing, hourly examinations were not returned to the students, a policy professor Ryan did not himself embrace. In fact, in other courses he taught, he posted the hourly examinations – complete with answers – outside the classroom while the test was being taken, and placed his previous test instruments for student access in the undergraduate library.

Not returning the hourly Accountancy 101 examinations prompted students to create a variety of schemes to get the test instruments, which changed little over the years. The large course enrollment meant some organized student residences had 10 or more residents enrolled in the course each semester, and each of them would be responsible for remembering two of the questions on a 20-question test. Back at the house, they would write out the questions, and after a couple of semesters, they had the entire examination in hand.

Since the Accountancy 101 classroom was filled beyond fire marshal standards, hourly examinations were given at night in the largest teaching auditorium on campus, where all doors, except those at the back, were locked. Students entered through the back doors, where they were required to show their identification cards and sign their names before taking a test instrument and then sitting in alternate seats in alternate rows. Numbered test instruments were returned along with correspondingly numbered answer sheets. Graduate students assisted in proctoring the examinations.

Members of the teaching team kept a copy of only the examinations to which they contributed questions or problems. With one exception. Tom Nathe – an attorney and previous member of the law school faculty who had opted to participate in international work and gave only a few lectures on business law – insisted on keeping a copy of every examination given by every instructor. Other team members lifted their eyebrows, but went along.

Professor Ryan became suspicious when two of his student advisees who were earning "Bs" and "Cs" in other courses made "As" in Accountancy 101. The remarkable grades for average students in a difficult course all went to women. Similar observations were made over the next three semesters.

The mystery was solved when one of professor Ryan's own advisees, Michelle Thomas, knocked on his office door late one afternoon. She was in an emotional state. Ryan invited Michelle to have a seat, and asked what he could do to help. "Just be my friend and listen," she replied. There ensued a burst of tears, but Michelle quickly swallowed them and began her story.

For years Michelle Thomas had dreamed of following in her grandfather's footsteps and studying the law. She had enjoyed a happy childhood, but her one consistent ambition was to join her Pawpaw's law firm. This had been her driving force to attend college in the first place. But aptitude test scores placed her in the middle of her peer group when it came to accountancy. Recognizing that the grade she received in Accountancy 101 would be crucial to fulfilling her plans, and realizing that one member of the teaching team was a former faculty member in the law college who just *had* to be – she reasoned – connected with the admission committee, Michelle Thomas turned to professor Tom Nathe for help.

At this point in her rendition, Michelle again began to cry. Her composure restored, she got to the nub of her story: Realizing her intense desire to become a practicing attorney, professor Nathe suggested that Michelle join him at his cabin, ten miles west of town, a beautiful setting in a wooded area overlooking the Manitou River. They could relax in a quiet and private environment and fully explore Michelle's dreams.

Feeling flattered but uncomfortable about the invitation, yet trusting her ability to control any situation that might arise, Michelle accepted Nathe's invitation to a counseling session two days later.

The retreat was all Tom Nathe had promised. And he quickly assured Michelle that, with her cooperation, he could arrange matters so her dream of obtaining a Juris Doctor degree would become reality. But there was a deal, a proposition, and Nathe was frank about it: sex in exchange for personal tutoring made possible by his having copies of the Accountancy 101 examinations.

This was wrong, and Michelle knew it. It went against her personal values and virtues. But she waffled. She let her confidence in Nathe's claimed ability to deliver on the thing most important to her – becoming an attorney – override her good judgment. She went along with the deal.

Now, Michelle confided to professor Ryan, every waking moment since that episode, she had had to deal with deep feelings of guilt. She had betrayed her parents, taken unfair advantage of her classmates, compromised the precepts she had so carefully outlined for herself. In short, she was confused, miserable, and ashamed.

Professor Ryan asked if there was anything he could do to help her. She responded, "I only hoped you would listen, and you have." He asked if she intended to press sexual-harassment charges. "I don't want to go through all that. It wouldn't change anything. Anyway, it would be his word against mine. Not good. I have to be responsible and learn to live with the wrong I did." She smiled a brave smile. "Thanks for listening. I must go now."

𝒮 𝒮 𝒮

Omnibus University offers numerous off-campus courses, conferences, workshops, and special programs for credit. Most are taught by resident faculty who receive special overload pay for their services. The rationale is to provide a mechanism for off-campus instruction on an as-needed basis.

For obvious reasons, there is always a waiting list of professors ready and willing to teach off-campus. For years, several faculty members at Omnibus taught essentially full-time off-campus. This, in effect, enabled them to earn nearly double pay for a normal teaching load, their only inconvenience being the travel associated with off-campus instruction. Since profit from the activity is shared with participating colleges and departments, deans and department heads encourage it, too.

What might appear to be a win-win program for everybody, however, frequently turns out otherwise. Ironically, the program victimizes resident students. In too many cases, rather than being taught by regular faculty – as should be expected at a comprehensive university – many students at the main campus are taught by part-time instructors who can be employed for lower salaries. On average, of course, these faculty members are also less professionally competent and experienced.

So, resident students are clear losers. But there are clear winners, too: the faculty who receive hefty salary supplements; departments and colleges that receive a portion of the profit generated, only part of which is needed to employ part-time instructors who serve as substitute teachers; and those who receive off-campus instruction by members of the resident faculty.

Higher education ... is out of control ... . Campuses are run for the benefit of the faculty ... increasingly out of touch with the rest of America, rejecting the culture of the people who pay their salaries ... . There is also an acceptance of higher costs without effective management by administrators.

Newt Gingrich (b. 1943)
To Renew America **(1995), p. 219**
Former history professor
Speaker, U.S. House of Representatives (1995-1999)

ℒ ℒ ℒ

Professor Lucas Terflinger "never met an insurance agent he didn't like". For sure, the insurance industry has never had a better friend than Luke Terflinger. For three decades, the tenured Omnibus professor of business – whose faculty contract called for teaching and research – has focused his efforts instead almost totally on direct service to insurance agents of all kinds, from one end of the state to the other.

Terflinger steadfastly has chosen to go against the academic tide. Many of his faculty colleagues and the administrators to whom he reports have not the foggiest notion of what makes the man tick, and they have mercilessly criticized him – as only a bunch of catty professors can do. One said that Luke Terflinger would rather serve as official scorekeeper at an insurance agents' horseshoe pitch than make love.

All this might have been okay – the professoriate benefits from diversity – but for a bevy of ugly facts. Professor Terflinger spends two-thirds of his work week off campus, tending the needs and problems he perceives the state's insurance agents are having. So, he neglects his contractual teaching responsibilities (nominally calling for three-quarters of his total effort), and has virtually abandoned his contractual research responsibilities (one quarter). He also illegally diverts university resources – ranging from using electricity, telephones, furniture, computers, furnaces, and air conditioners, not to mention secretarial services, to duping students into doing association work under the guise of "special problems" and "independent study" courses.

It has happened more than once: just about the time the associate director of the business school has cranked up his courage and assigned a course to Terflinger to teach – just when he thinks he has Terflinger earning some of his university salary for a change – Luke Terflinger, the guy who can not say "no" to an insurance agent, agrees to serve as interim executive secretary of another insurance agents' association of some sort and begs off the teaching assignment. In twenty-five years, he has served the casualty insurance agents, auto insurance representatives, and IRA salespeople of the state as a paid, part-time, so-called interim staffer for a total of thirteen years, seven straight one time.

There can be honest debate over whether what rings professor Lucas Terflinger's chime is legitimate university work. But one thing is certain: Neglecting his responsibilities as teacher and adviser of students cannot be forgiven. Every time Luke Terflinger cashes a salary check drawn on Omnibus University's payroll account, he should be shame-filled. But somehow he rationalizes his behavior. Although his mind has been elsewhere 90 percent of the time for over a quarter of a century, he derives great pleasure and security from the job protection of tenure's safety net.

> The arguments against tenure are stronger by far than any in favor of it.
>
> **Jay Parini (b. 1948)**
> **Author, biographer, and**
> **professor at Middlebury College**

𝒮 𝒮 𝒮

As counterpoint to professor Lucas Terflinger, Dr. Steven Zimbalist, a sixth-year Omnibus University assistant professor of applied economics, takes his teaching responsibilities seriously. His contract calls for 80 percent of his effort to come in teaching. By usual norms, it actually stands at around 120 percent. Zimbalist is a nationally recognized authority on food-service economics, and spends many hours every week on the telephone keeping in touch with the food-service industry and then – after processing what he has learned – being interviewed by the editors of food-service trade newspapers and magazines. As might be guessed, he is a whiz at analyzing and integrating what he has learned, and trade journalists have learned that, when they consult Steven Zimbalist, he makes them look smart.

And what does Zimbalist get in return? Not gifts. His scruples are such that he never accepts any gift of any kind from industry or publisher – not so much as a cold Coke on a hot day.

Whereas professor Terflinger may go a whole week sitting in his office but accomplishing nothing under his Omnibus contract, Zimbalist is made of a different cut of cloth. He invariably hustles as he stands in the classroom, as he strides purposefully from place to place in the library, as he sits in front of his powerful, globally networked microcomputer.

Almost all students in the courses professor Zimbalist teaches relate well with him, and so they learn much under his encouragement and guidance. Already after his fourth year on the faculty, Zimbalist's peers and students recognized him as the college's outstanding teacher of the year.

But recently an ugly fly landed on Steve Zimbalist's ointment, and it could have cost him his job. Some of his full-professor, traditionalist, do-it-one-way-our-way peers believe an assistant professor should consistently publish at least one peer-reviewed economics paper every year, and they were stubbornly disinclined to change their view. Anything less or other than one journal paper a year struck them as insufficient scholarly activity for one to be promoted to associate-professor rank and granted academic tenure. In six years at Omnibus, Zimbalist has published only four papers in peer-reviewed economics journals.

Steve Zimbalist is a practical, pragmatic fellow, and says he simply finds that most weeks he has very little time left which can be devoted to the sort of research and writing involved in developing peer-reviewed papers. His scholarship efforts – everyone agrees – go in other directions, and for as far as they go, they are excellent.

> Our troubled planet can no longer afford the luxury of pursuits confined to an ivory tower. Scholarship has to prove its worth, not on its own terms, but by service to the nation and the world.
>
> **Oscar Handlin (b. 1915)**
> **Professor Emeritus, Harvard University**

Those traditionalists in his midst recently were on the brink of turning Steven Zimbalist's office light off forever. But Arts and Sciences dean Simon Solomon came to his rescue. The dean had been contacted by heavy-hitters from the state food-processing and restaurant association when they caught wind of the malarkey hitting Steve Zimbalist's promotion-and-tenure fan. The dean agreed with his visitors, and proceeded to remind members of the college promotion-and-tenure committee of an Omnibus professor decades earlier who had very much the same sort of record of productivity as Dr. Zimbalist. His name was Anthony Adams Ainsworth, and he was protected and salvaged from that era's promotion-and-tenure committee's trash heap by a savvy, salty, sage president who, upon hearing of Ainsworth's predicament, called the committee chair to his office and asked him about the case: "What the heck is going on here anyway?" Adams Ainsworth was promoted and tenured, and eventually went on to become arguably Omnibus's strongest president this century.

Similarly, soon after Simon Solomon's remarks at the college committee meeting, Dr. Steven Zimbalist found himself newly appointed an associate professor with academic tenure.

> The prime business of American professors must be regular, assiduous class teaching.
>
> **Charles William Elliott (1834-1926)**
> **American educator**

REMEMBERING ... *The Tales of Two Students*

The College Board has reported that in the past 15 years the average cost of attending private colleges has increased by 90 percent, and the average for public institutions by 100 percent. At the same time, median family income has risen just 5 percent ... colleges should cut administrative costs more effectively. While undergraduate enrollment increased 28 percent from 1975 to 1993, non-teaching administrative positions grew by 83 percent.

Stephen Burd
"Colleges Ask for Relief from 'Unrelenting' Government Rules"
The Chronicle of Higher Education, **July 26, 1996, p. A35**

The past two decades have seen not only explosive growth in the cost of college but a dramatic change in who pays. From 1974 to 1994, the average cost of four years of tuition, room, board, and fees at public universities rose from $11,032 to $25,785. Private school costs went from $25,514 to $64,410.

Joshua Wolf Shenk, *US News & World Report*, **June 9, 1997, p. 38**

To avoid heavy debt, an increasing number of students work full-time while attending college. These students cannot carry a full course load at the same time, so many are taking six or more years to graduate.... . Increasing tuition and the shift of federal student-aid money from grants to loans have forced students to take out more loans than ever, and many students realize only after their first year that they cannot manage the debt.

Mary Geraghty, "Data Show More Students
Quitting College Before Sophomore Year"
The Chronicle of Higher Education, **July 19, 1996, p. A35-36**

The best form of financial aid is low tuition.

Melanie B. Cruz, President, Student Government Association
University of Kentucky-Lexington *Kentucky Kernel*
October 30, 1997, p. 1

Some college administrators readily admit that the single most important factor in setting tuition is an estimation of what the wealthiest families might be willing to pay.

Herbert London
John M. Olin Professor of Humanities, New York University
Tulsa World, **April 1, 1998, p. A-18**

CHAPTER 6

INSTITUTIONAL CULTURE:
CRONYISM, NEPOTISM, FEATHERBEDS

Each institution has a way of life – a tradition, a set of
values, a pattern of customs – that influences and provides a
framework for the educational experiences of members of a
campus community.

Mary Ellen Chase (1887-1973)
American educator and author

Ellen and Perry Fairchild were full-time employees of
Omnibus University. Ellen clerked in the History Department.
Perry oversaw the maintenance of the performing arts center facilities. Both were conscientious workers who continually tried
to increase their own efficiency and productivity as well as that
of the institution. Unfortunately, as the Fairchilds learned, the
culture of Omnibus did not necessarily favor enhanced
efficiency and productivity.

The Fairchilds had strong commitments to full
accountability for public funds. Perry observed the superfluous
layers of supervisors in his part of the university operation; far
more employees than needed. Frustrated by the inaction of his
immediate supervisor, he wrote a letter to the vice-president for
operations, pointing out the waste of labor in the maintenance

and operations division, calling for review and remedy. Why should the local taxpaying citizenry not be disgusted, he asked, when they see Omnibus vehicles all over campustown all day long as employees take extended breaks at doughnut shops, restaurants, and fast-food outlets? He suggested a study be made to find ways and means of eliminating redundancy and featherbedding, and the layers upon layers of administrators and supervisors. About a week later, Perry was called by his immediate supervisor, who mentioned the letter and implored him either to be a team player and go along with *status quo* or to leave. Not having another job with such pay, benefits, and security to turn to, Perry waffled. He compromised his commitment to accountability. He went along so he could get along. He had a chance to take a moral stand, but he muffed it.

Ellen admitted that the work she was assigned could be done in two hours each day. Her sense of guilt grew and her self-esteem shrank. Ellen told her supervisor about her feelings. From her work area, she said, any direction she looked she saw underworked clerical employees who spent less time performing official duties than reading novels and newspapers, clipping coupons, writing personal letters, making out checks to pay bills, engaging in extended personal telephone conversations, and taking lengthy breaks in the lounge and coffee room. The supervisor's response was to facilitate Ellen's transfer to another unit. Ellen said that, if it would result in more meaningful employment, she would welcome such a change.

She was transferred. But again, apart from taking telephone messages, her responsibilities could be accomplished by mid-morning each day. Ellen's work ethic, desire to be accountable for compensation received, and general disgust with an institutional culture more intent on increasing student tuition and fees and legislative handouts than on cutting costs and boosting efficiency, eventually took her to the breaking point. She chose the moral high road, resigned her cozy position, and returned to part-time employment. Ellen's action made her feel better about herself. It also made it easier for the Fairchilds to rationalize Perry's morally lame decision.

꽃 꽃 꽃

Gilbert Mabry grew up in a blue-collar family in an industrial city on the western state line. He worked his way through
Omnibus University, graduating thirtysome years ago with a
degree in accounting and business. Gib Mabry never left
Omnibus. He was working part-time in the College of Education
business office the year before graduation. The week after
graduation, the position had become full-time, and he has
worked in the same office suite ever since.

Gib Mabry, master survivor, has outlasted four deans, sev-
enteen department heads and program directors, four vice-presidents for business, and three newfangled accounting systems,
and he has weathered many a political storm, as well. Along the
way, he has been promoted several times, most recently, over a
decade ago, to college business manager.

No one better understands than Mabry the state fiscal stat-
utes, university finance policies, and college business
operations; certainly not any of those deans, every one of whom
was, as Gib puts it, "an import". Upon assuming their duties, to
the person, each dean in turn immediately depended on Gib
Mabry to protect them from being scalded by financial hot
water. Of course, the deans had plenty of other matters to tend,
and almost every day Mabry reassured them in their laxity when
he would tell them, "All's well so far today on the bean-countin'
front, dean. You just go on now and worry 'bout your other
things."

This would have been okay if Gib Mabry had only stuck to
business procedures. But over the years, he became more and
more adventurous and started dabbling in academic policy. With
a succession of deans, every one of whom lacked training and
experience in business procedures and finance, Mabry became
not only the chief executive officer's protector and sounding
board but one of his primary advisers, as well, a role that was
not part of the business manager's job description. Savvy
department heads and even individual faculty and staff members
knew that Mabry's nod of approval was tantamount to the

dean's, so they curried the favor of this fellow who was already watching over the college money bags before many of them had finished grade school. The result: academic policy was being set *de facto* by a nonacademic staffer.

A college business manager is hired to ensure that public funds are being used in efficient, legal ways. The academic matters Gib Mabry made his business might have needed attention, but they simply were not his business.

Current education dean Ronny Hardin's heart and soul lie in reorienting the college's direction for the future – big-picture matters – not minding the daily nitty-gritty of the financial books. So he greatly depends on Mabry, who does not miss a chance to meddle, holding more sway with Hardin than he has with any earlier dean. For one thing, Mabry was middle-aged when Santa Claus was a boy, and the dean is the sort who respects, as he puts it, "the wisdom that comes with years".

Recently, Mabry started barraging Hardin with suggestions about how to run the laboratory school. He argued, for example, that completing the college computer network should enjoy higher priority than remodeling the laboratory-school cafeteria. Never mind that the laboratory school has a director, Dr. Thelma Hughes. Hardin hears Mabry's views on the school several times most days, those of Hughes only a couple of times a week. Over time, slowly, surely, the dean came to honor the business manager's advice more than the school director's, setting the stage for a huge clash.

Gib Mabry's spouse has been a fifth-grade teacher in the local schools off and on since before they were married, and of course he himself was a student once. In his opinion, these experiences give him special insights into the management of the laboratory school. Never mind that his ideas were obsolete and ignored the fact that the laboratory school has dual objectives – educating classroom students and educating apprentice teachers – and therefore cannot be run as a public school is.

Director Hughes felt betrayed by her dean, who gave unending lip service to her opinions, but routinely undercut her by siding with Mabry in terms of expectations. One day, at a dust-settling meeting ordered but not attended by the dean, Hughes told Mabry she would like never again to hear him refer to how things are done in the local school system and thus should be done in the laboratory school, reminding him that academic policy was none of the business manager's business.

In the end, might meant right, and college business manager Gilbert Mabry survived while laboratory school director Thelma Hughes was "relieved of administrative duties" and returned to the professoriate.

When word of Hughes's treatment got around the country, no individuals of strong professional stature could be persuaded by two director search committees in a row to even visit Omnibus, let alone apply for the directorship of the laboratory school. After over two years of interim directors, dean Ronny Hardin recommended that one of his former graduate students (whose career had stalled as an associate professor years earlier) be appointed to the position. The provost swiftly did just that.

℣ ℣ ℣

Cronyism – the habitual practice of hiring friends, epitomizing the "good-ol'-boy" syndrome – and nepotism – showing favoritism in hiring relatives on the basis of relationship – are rampant all across Omnibus University. Examples will prove the point.

℣ Omnibus University has a stated commitment to any new faculty member that a spouse may pursue doctoral studies at Omnibus. Moreover, when the doctorate is awarded, the university promises to appoint the new graduate to a tenure-track faculty position in an appropriate discipline, sometimes even in the same department as the new hiree. Of course, this practice precludes even the possibility of appointing better qualified or more experienced people in those positions. Nepotism is especially troubling in cases where both spouses are engaged in the same discipline and employed in the same unit. Over time, it usually weakens the quality of that faculty.

ॐ   Another situation at Omnibus has been permitted to evolve and fester for many years. More than two-thirds of the staff members hired in a critical student-services area are relatives of existing staffers. When a position vacancy occurs, the office leader – who inherited the position from her father – appoints a committee to evaluate applicants and recommend an appointee. Sometimes, every member of one of these committees is related to all others. Invariably, the committee recommends yet another relative or, if none has applied, a close friend of one or more of the people already on the staff. The most important selection criterion is not professional skills and expertise, but rather how well the applicant will "fit-in".

ॐ   In a third case, the head of an academic department was permitted to hire her spouse as an academic adviser. He turned out to be unfamiliar with and uninterested in learning the sequencing of required courses in the secondary-education curriculum. This resulted in his giving poor counsel to many students, who as a consequence had to enroll at Omnibus an additional semester or two to complete course requirements for their degrees.

   Examples of cronyism abound in the awarding of scholarships to sons and daughters of special friends as well as internal grants to faculty members.

ॐ   In one case, a senior administrator became amorously involved with his secretary, took her on business trips, gave her obscenely large salary increases as well as big bottles of his favorite fragrance, and in time arranged for a unique graduate-study program that led to her earning a doctorate from Omnibus University at the same time as she was receiving full salary and benefits. Upon completing the Ph.D. degree, a special administrative position was created for the woman – one that paid 65 percent more than that paid the average new tenure-track assistant professor.

🦥 In a second example, Malcomb Russell, the trustees' trustee, asked an Omnibus vice-president to create a lucrative position to accommodate employment of a son of a close friend from trustee Russell's boyhood. Of course, the vice-president did so.

🦥 A high-ranking administrator fished, hunted, and socialized with a nontenured employee-friend. When this friend's position had to be eliminated because external funding fizzled out, the administrator quickly "found" funds to support his buddy, a person who had neither professional expertise nor training in the area of the new position. This came just five months after the same administrator had created another brand-new position for the spouse of a local attorney-state legislator.

🦥 🦥 🦥

In a way, it is a shame that Bob Miller's undergraduate professors at Omnibus University – who straight away saw the young man's brains and talents – selfishly ignored what would have been best for him. Instead, they urged him to stay on at Omnibus for graduate studies. Miller, in particular, would have benefited from experiencing a broader horizon, from learning there is more than the Omnibus way to achieve any objective. But stay at Omnibus to earn two more degrees in ceramic engineering is exactly what Bob Miller did. Then, to exacerbate Miller's academic myopia, Omnibus stumbled again. It wooed and hired him right out of its graduate-student ranks to serve on its faculty.

More often than not, such situations lead to an assistant professor whom older professors have trouble respecting as a faculty colleague. But Bob Miller was a special case. He immediately put his claw marks high up on the trees all around the department, in fact, everywhere there was a department storeroom.

Miller's first week on the job, the department head and half the faculty had gone – as they had every summer for two decades – to fish in the Minnesota-Ontario boundary waters. The brash new recruit seized the moment and spent the week going through the department storerooms, carting to the dumpster anything that had no name on it or that he considered nonessential.

It was not that the storerooms did not need purging. People talked all the time about doing it. But in the ivory tower, it simply is rarely, if ever, done. When thirty-year-veteran professor Axel Storm stuck his head in a storeroom and asked assistant professor Bob Miller what he was doing, the neophyte looked the man who had taught him junior engineering practice straight in the eye and answered with a question, "What does it look like?"

Head secretary Phyllis Hosimer alerted her spouse, Wally, a union steward in the physical plant, to what was going on. When Wally Hosimer dropped in to inform the young professor that the Teamsters had a labor contract to do all the carting on campus, Bob Miller simply changed his workday schedule to start at 4 p.m. each afternoon, after most physical plant employees had turned in their keys and tools and minivans for the day.

There was grousing for a couple of weeks after the fishing party returned from the northlands to find the department storerooms tidied up and then some. But it soon blew over. And then, in Bob Miller's case, something strange happened. From that point on, Miller was respected as a full-fledged faculty member, his path never blocked, his chin whiskers rarely tweaked.

In fact, for over 30 years, the super-aggressive Bob Miller – the most highly inbred of academic creatures – terrorized every faculty and staff member in his home department, ceramic engineering. He had plenty going for himself, at least in the beginning, but constantly compared and contrasted his approaches and accomplishments with those of everybody else. Calumny, innuendo, and invective became his favorite tools, as he mastered building himself up by tearing others down. When he told the department machinist to always give Miller Group jobs first priority, the machinist never questioned his authority to give such an audacious and outrageous order.

Before long, no one – faculty, staff, or student – had the temerity to challenge or question Dr. Bob Miller about anything. If he said black was white, a few people in the room nodded, most sat stock still, none shook heads, cleared throats, or raised eyebrows. They all had seen or at least heard about the claw marks Miller left on the storeroom trees his first week as an assistant professor.

So, as Bob Miller developed as a faculty member, he had a void in his experience. He never had to match wits with anyone; never lost a debate; soon came to believe he could think, say, or write no wrong. His graduate students and technicians agreed.

This approach worked successfully around Omnibus for many years. But away from the place, Miller gained a reputation for conducting unimaginative research. When a student of his bragged about Big Daddy's published-paper output the year before, one scientist remarked, "Can't have been much to most of them." In the end, Miller's was a reputation for conducting scads of experiments employing an approach that an Omnibus predecessor had invented 15 years earlier, and from which Miller glibly extracted generalizations. Indeed, most of the results amounted to little. Also, Miller's was a reputation for using a cookie cutter to shape graduate students. After graduation, these look-alike academic siblings tended to do well so long as they were close enough to Big Daddy to reflect his brilliance. Once they grabbed for their own rings in the real world, however, they tended to fizzle and sputter.

Academic scholarship is supposed to work this way: A scholar puts forward an idea or a proposition; shares the evidence, justification, or reasoning; then defends it against a barrage of challenging questions by appropriately cynical fellow scientists. When a scientist's peers fail to test his assertions and claims, they are abrogating their responsibility, and the scientist – and especially the scientist's students – are being shortchanged. Dr. Bob Miller never got the point. He retired believing his way, the Omnibus way, was the only way.

❦ ❦ ❦

Harpy Harpster grew up in the shadow of the Omnibus greenhouse. The only thing he ever wanted to do was follow in the footsteps of his great-uncle, Harpy Harpster, the floriculture specialist level III at Omnibus for 40 years. As a schoolboy, Harpy the younger spent much of his spare time tagging along with Harpy the elder, who timed his own retirement so his great-nephew could take his place, a scheme that brought tears to the eyes and nostrils and quivers to the chin of trustee Sallie Snell-Schumacher.

The younger Harpy had a thing about African violets. Since he was ten years old, he had cultivated as many as 150 varieties at home. When all the window ledges had been filled, his Grand-father Harpster, Harpy the elder's older brother, came one Satur-day and put up automatic grow-light and watering systems in a corner of the basement, with space for at least 300 pots.

By the time young Harpy was 12, he was winning African violet shows at the state level. At 15 his Georgia Ruby specimen won best of show at the National African Violet Exposition in Kansas City. African violets were in Harpy Harpster's blood from then on.

Several people twice his age – and having scads more edu-cation and experience – bid for the job. With Harpy the elder's connections coming through in fine Omnibus fashion, however, Harpy the younger assumed management of the Omnibus green-house and trial gardens at age nineteen, after just one year of post-high-school apprenticeship with his great-uncle.

Unlike his great-uncle, who was a selfless, service-oriented staff member, Harpy the younger's first love, again, was African violets. He cared little about or for the other 170-some species of plant material the professors' teaching and research programs required. He never said as much, but the sorry condition of most of those other plants most of the time spoke loud and clear.

When a professor wanted to know why the plants were not healthier, young Harpy had more than enough excuses to send the faculty member away mumbling to the ground. When a professor complained about young Harpy's ways to the faculty member who oversaw the greenhouse and gardens, no help was forthcoming, partly no doubt because the professor-in-charge was Harpy the elder's son-in-law. And when the complaint was registered at the next level, again nothing much ever happened, partly no doubt because the department head had been the doctoral-study adviser of the son-in-law-professor-in-charge.

In time, Harpy Harpster the younger became the winningest fancier and most productive amateur hybridizer in the 200-year history of the United States African Violet League. He had a modest greenhouse at home that served as a sham operation. His cultivation and hybridization action took place right in the open, if you knew what you were looking for, on Omnibus time, on Omnibus property, using Omnibus equipment and supplies and Omnibus student workers. Weekly he had specimens – express-shipped in Omnibus soil in Omnibus pots in Omnibus shock-mounted, insulated, shipping containers – entered in several shows all over North America. Some years, Harpy Harpster's income from shows and hybrid-licensing exceeded his Omnibus salary two times over.

Needless to say, the students of professors who wanted to use African violets in research or teaching never had access to anything but the plants Harpy had rejected because they were diseased or stunted or some such.

On only one occasion did Harpy's modus operandi come under serious attack. The taxpayer-mother of a student worker who knew the score wrote a letter of complaint to the chair of the Omnibus board of trustees. The current holder of the Snell seat on the board volunteered to look into the charges. At the next meeting, Sallie Snell-Schumacher reported finding no evidence to support the charges that had been leveled at Harpy the younger. She recommended that the board executive secretary send the taxpayer-mother a letter saying just that. The motion was seconded and passed, and the board moved right on to the next item on its agenda.

𝒮 𝒮 𝒮

Will Maull was a four-decade employee of Omnibus University. Over the years he had great success in obtaining external funds for his favorite work-related pursuit – international development – enjoying an abundance of experiences traveling abroad.

Early on, Will learned that by delaying purchase of airline tickets till a few days before departure there just might be no economy coach seats remaining so, following university policy, he could purchase first-class tickets. He also learned to enjoy delays en route – "time-zone adjustments", he called them – in places such as California and Hawaii. And he learned that the promise of international junkets made it possible to gain loyalty and personal favors from all kinds of people.

For example, Will's relationship with Hillary Zany, who was experiencing mid-life rough waters in her marriage at the time, flourished. Hillary's spouse was director of placement at the university and scheduled numerous weekend treks off-campus to screen prospective employers. Hillary suspected nothing until the day she was going through his toilet kit looking for dental floss and ran across glow-in-the-dark condoms. Nothing he could say would quell her anxiety and suspicion.

When Hillary Zany broke down and shared her personal concerns with Will Maull, he quickly detected her desire to get even, and offered to take her along on an upcoming site visit to an international project. He would simply cash in some frequent flier points to purchase her ticket. Hillary was thrilled, accepted the invitation, and planned accordingly.

The plans materialized, and the stopover in Hawaii went so well it was extended a couple of days – for the record – to confer with a professional contact on the Big Island.

The special relationship between Hillary and Will became the talk of the office. This was amplified one noon hour when all employees, except those two, got together and took lunch at a campustown pizzeria. Monica Wheeler, a busybody staffer who had a nose for trouble, made an excuse to return to the office early. When she burst unannounced into Will Maull's inner office, she found both Hillary and Will in a partial state of undress, she astraddle and facing him, sitting in his high-backed chair, coupled in a profound embrace.

This episode, of course, put the two lovers in compromising positions. So Will soon offered Monica Wheeler a promotion and salary increase as hush incentives. When she refused the offer, she was asked to resign. It was at this point that she made an appointment to confer with university president Burton Cromley.

Monica Wheeler shared numerous insights with president Cromley, including knowledge of Will Maull's concurrent purchase of two pickup trucks – one for an overseas project, one for his personal use. For the university project, he purchased a model that had virtually every accessory available. Moreover, she knew from reading letters from the overseas project manager that the pickup's steering wheel was on the left and could not be licensed for highway use in the project country. She was aware, too, that by paying the full suggested sticker price on the university vehicle, the dealer had given Will an extraordinarily huge discount on his personal pickup.

Monica Wheeler also reported that Maull had purchased from the same dealer a California-class field disk at full cost for an overseas project in order to benefit from an extra-large discount on a camper to go on his own new pickup truck. And she knew, again through subsequent correspondence, that the disk had been too large for the small tractors and draft animals available on most of the farms in the project country. Even for tractors powerful enough to pull the disk, it was too large to turn around on the small experimental plots. The disk went unused, and time and again was cited by the locals as a monumental budget-breaking, bureaucratic booboo.

Monica Wheeler also noted for president Cromley that Will Maull called his daughter frequently on his university telephone, and had made no offer to make payment on over a thousand dollars charged to project accounts the past two years. President Cromley assured Wheeler he would look into the matter. Since the university had monthly accountings of each telephone line, it was a simple matter to check the long distance calls Maull was making. Sure enough, there were charges for calls to his daughter's telephone, totaling over a thousand dollars the past two years alone.

President Cromley decided to discuss the matter with Hosea Joiner, executive secretary to the governing board, the procedure the board had instructed Cromley to follow. But the spineless Hosea Joiner – a highly paid staff administrator who was actually nothing more than a puppet manipulated by board member Malcomb Russell, who had personally seen to his being hired years earlier – had once worked for Will Maull. That fact and personal friendship, coupled with his knowledge of Will's having taken several board members – including Malcomb Russell and Frank Drysdale – on long trips, plus the knowledge that they would be supportive of Will, caused Hosea Joiner to rationalize that the matter was "small potatoes", and bringing it to surface would cause embarrassment for the institution. He quickly concluded that the best approach would be to simply sweep it under the rug. This was done, in spite of president Cromley's mild objection.

Ironically, in a subsequent chapter, within a year, board executive secretary Hosea Joiner caused praise to be heaped upon Will Maull through official board of trustees recognition of his long-term, dedicated service to Omnibus University.

𝔙 𝔙 𝔙

The campus culture at Omnibus University is resolutely anti-change. When a change is proposed, the standard response is: "Hey, we've *always* done it this way – and even before that."

𝔙 The clinging-to-the-past syndrome may involve, for example, a proposed change in the circulation of a particular edition of *Current Contents* among faculty members in a given discipline – a practice that often required six or more months for an issue to make the rounds from the campus library across the desks of dozens of faculty (with individual delays frequently exceeding two weeks) and back to the shelves of the library, where it would be accessible to the rest of the university community.

With the advent of modern electronic technology, it was determined that it would be simpler and more efficient to access *Current Contents* via CD-ROM from the offices of individual faculty members. But when it was proposed that circulating the publication be stopped, an influential faculty member reminded the library advisory committee that "it's always been done this way".

Investigation revealed that a former professor of considerable renown, now deceased for over fifteen years, had some three decades earlier caused the *Current Contents* circulation practice to be instituted as one of his demands for silence when he found his spouse in a compromising relationship with the university librarian.

🎵 Another example of honoring the past at the expense of present-day efficiency involved providing two sets of facilities and instructional staffs to teach languages. One language laboratory facility was located in the English Department, and it had its own faculty and team of teaching assistants. A similar laboratory and staff was located in the Classics Department. When a faculty-student committee reviewed the situation and recommended that the two facilities and staffs be merged to help standardize instruction, improve operating efficiency, and reduce costs, the proposal was met with a loud, collective outcry from those involved, who said: "But we've always done it this way."

🎵 Then there is copious unnecessary paperwork. For example, before an Omnibus faculty member can submit a research paper for publication in a scientific journal, it has to have the written approval of his or her section leader, department head, the associate dean for research, the dean, the head of the grants and contracts office, the university legal counsel, the public information officer, and the vice-president for research. Few if any of the persons providing (mostly by proxy) the eight required signatures read the paper, and those who do probably would not understand it. Indeed, most of those who do the actual signing are secretaries. So why go through the time-consuming, wasteful process? Mainly because "we've always done it this way".

∽ ∽ ∽

Nearly all men can stand adversity, but if you want to test a man's character, give him power.
Abraham Lincoln (1809-1865)
Sixteenth President, United States of America

Amy Adams had dreamed since she was eight of becoming a veterinarian. Now she knew she could successfully compete for admission to veterinary school. Amy had loved animals for as long as she could remember. She had read all of James Herriott's books. And she had enjoyed every moment spent on her grandparents' farm, where she experienced the personal satisfaction of becoming friends with many animals.

As a National Merit Finalist graduating in the upper one percent of a large high school class, Amy Adams received several scholarships to attend Omnibus, where she earned straight As. Then came the Veterinary Aptitude Test; Amy ranked in the 99th percentile nationally.

Amy's faculty adviser, Dr. Haley Herman, experienced in counseling pre-veterinary students, had recommended a rigorous plan of study to prepare her for the challenges of professional school. After reading her application, Dr. Herman gave Amy a smile. "I'm very proud of you," he said.

After some weeks, Amy received the letter she had been hoping for, inviting her for an interview with the veterinary admission committee. From her perspective, the meeting went well. Committee members had asked the right questions and Amy had interacted freely.

The period between interview and receipt of her notification letter seemed long. But Amy moved confidently through those days, thinking "no news is good news".

The wait came to an abrupt end when a colleague of Amy's father advised him that, through the grapevine, he had learned that Amy was going to be denied admission to the Omnibus veterinary college. The word was that Amy needed time to mature.

Although the news was unofficial, Amy's father decided to shift into action. By the time Amy actually received the notification letter, her father had the necessary information and legal counsel to inform the dean of veterinary medicine, Dr. Walter Windham, that a federal class-action law suit would be filed on behalf of the many women applicants who had been discriminated against.

As it turned out, admission was dictated by the dean, who had his own criteria and made a mockery of the faculty's admission index. And Amy's father and attorneys had learned that there were more than 70 women applicants who had been assigned index total scores that were higher than the score of the lowest male applicant admitted. Moreover, through cooperative veterinary college staffers, her lawyers learned that Amy's total score (based on criteria established by the selection committee itself) was the highest for any woman and tied for highest overall.

The dean was obviously concerned by the situation, although apparently not because of any injustices, but rather because his unprofessional, unethical, illegal practices might now be openly scrutinized. His ineptness soon became apparent when, through one of his assistant deans, Dr. Thelen Westbrook, he asked the faculty member in charge of all admission-related data, Dr. Julian Bedford, to destroy the computer printouts of applicant index scores. Dr. Bedford made no commitment to the dean, but instead, employed private legal counsel. His attorney advised him to destroy no evidence. Later, these data were subpoenaed in the discovery phase of the law suit. Careful review revealed a bias in favor of male applicants. Moreover, they showed irregularities in the admission of male applicants, too.

What motivated dean Windham to intervene and selectively admit individual applicants? In Amy Adams's case, dean Windham bore a grudge against the applicant's father. Both men bred and showed Sealyham terriers, and for several years American Kennel Club judges had been in the habit of placing Adams's entries ahead of Windham's in the show ring.

The rumor mill shifted into overdrive with regard to this brewing gender-discrimination case. Only later did it come out that the university's chief legal counsel advised dean Windham that his decisions related to admission were indefensible, and that he should hope several applicants already admitted would decline, providing the opportunity to revisit Amy Adams's application. Two students did decline their acceptance, and the dean quickly advised Amy Adams that she had been admitted.

Amy Adams's troubles did not end when her veterinary studies began. Following the first and second round of veterinary school examinations, on which Amy set the class curve, the first-year-student president asked Amy to purposefully give wrong answers so as to lower the spread between her grades and those of the rest of the students. If Amy did not cooperate, she could expect to be bitten when classmates would "accidentally" release their hold on dogs being restrained for examination. Also, Amy was cautioned that if she did not heed his warning, she might find the parking lot to be an unsafe place at night when she left to go home. These threats concerned Amy Adams, but she would not compromise her integrity.

Adding to this pressure was assistant dean Westbrook's request of her. He told Amy that her curve-setting grades were causing problems among lower-performing students in the class. With that, Amy volunteered to mentor these students at night and on weekends.

Amy Adams graduated in veterinary medicine "with highest distinction", and carried the class banner across the stage at commencement ceremonies. Following graduation, she completed internship and residency programs in two of the nation's leading veterinary colleges before accepting a faculty position at another distinguished institution. She was board-certified in two specialties and has contributed to the training of veterinary students as well as the development of her subdisciplines through research. And, she currently chairs the admission committee for the college of veterinary medicine where she works.

As long as the world shall last there will be wrongs, and if no man objected and no man rebelled, those wrongs would last forever.
Clarence Darrow (1857-1938)
American trial lawyer and author

Honor never grows old, and honor gives the greatest joy, because honor is, finally, about defending noble and worthy things that deserve to be defended, even at a high cost.
William J. Bennett (b. 1943)
United States Secretary of Education (1985-1988)
Current Co-Director, Empower America
Fellow, Heritage Foundation

Too many people put in "face time". They show up for work, and think that's good enough. Many even believe that they're working hard.
Judith M. Bardwick (b. 1933)
Danger in the Comfort Zone, **AMACOM Books, 1991**
American Management Association

REMEMBERING ... *The Tales of Two Students*

McGeorge Bundy (1919-1996), former President of the Ford Foundation (1966-1979), stirred considerable discussion when, in the Foundation's 1966 annual report, he was critical of existing attitudes and practices in the management of educational endowments. The study, Managing Educational Endowments, published by the Foundation in 1969, made a strong case for professional investment management ... .

John F. Meck, Founding President, The Common Fund

With tuition rates soaring, family income stagnating, and the purchasing power of the Pell Grant plummeting over the past 15 years, fewer and fewer of the neediest young people are going to college, experts on financial aid say. Those who do are finding their options increasingly limited to community colleges.

**Stephen Burd, "Some Educators Say Democrats
Have Deserted Low-Income Students"**
The Chronicle of Higher Education, **October 18, 1996, p. A27**

Everyone knows that students have to get higher education and so, in a sense, it's a seller's market. I worry that there are less incentives for them to think about ways in which they can reduce those costs to provide the educational needs of students and, at the same time, keep down the overall costs of running these institutions.

**Christopher Dodd, U.S. Senator, Connecticut
"Congress, Education Officials at Odds on College Cost Controls"**
USA Today, **May 29, 1997, pg. 10D**

Colleges and universities are turning their backs on the principle of meeting financial need as they adopt programs, such as merit aid, that are aimed mainly at more affluent students. It is increasingly clear ... that, unchecked, this trend will lead to growing stratification in U.S. higher education and increasing inequality of income and opportunity in society at large.

**Michael McPherson, President, MacAlester College
"College Aid Often Goes to Well-Off"**, *Columbia Daily Tribune*
February 18, 2000, p. 72

Public anxiety about college prices has risen along with increases in tuition ... members of the commission are ... convinced that if this public concern continues, and if colleges and universities do not take steps to reduce their costs, policymakers at the federal and state levels will intervene and take up the task for them.

**"Straight Talk About College Costs and Prices"
January 1998 report of 11-member National Commission
appointed by the US Congress in accordance with
Public Law 105-18 (Title IV, Cost of Higher Education Review, 1997)**

CHAPTER 7

INSTITUTIONAL CULTURE: FRAUD, DECEIT, CONSPIRACY

> If a million people do a foolish thing, it is still a foolish thing.
>
> **Jacques Anatole (1844-1924)**
> **French novelist and satirist**

Dr. Felix Schultz, a full professor at Omnibus University, enjoyed a worldwide reputation in computer science that enabled him, over the years, to gather millions of dollars of research grants and contracts from the United States Department of Defense, the National Aeronautics and Space Administration, industrial firms, and private foundations. Since his research involved considerable international travel, he had a good working relationship with the manager of Collegeville's most prominent travel agency. Although hard to believe, over the years, Felix Schultz devised a slick way to move money from his externally-funded research accounts into his personal travel account.

Schultz would process requests for university travel advances and airfare payments. At a precise point in time, he would cancel the trip and order his travel agency to transfer the money already paid to his personal travel account. Later he would use these personal-account funds to pay for airfares connected with consulting and guest-lecturing. When these sponsors provided reimbursements of their own, Schultz would pocket the proceeds. Some of these personal-account monies were even used to pay airfare for members of his family.

This nefarious scheme enabled professor Felix Schultz to personally benefit to the tune of more than a quarter million dollars over almost two decades of theft and deceit. When word of the scheme leaked out into the general community, it had been bad for business, so the owner of the travel agency – ignoring the advice of university administrators – demanded action from the state attorney general to clear her company's name. The professor was prosecuted and sent to prison.

✍ ✍ ✍

Charmaine Schelling – an attractive, personable extrovert – was a four-year cheerleader and two-time homecoming queen in high school. Her wealthy paternal grandmother bought her expensive clothes, real jewels, a new sports car at sixteen, photographic equipment, musical instruments, numerous trips abroad. Classmates envied Charmaine.

Charmaine Schelling's academic achievements were notable, as well. She ranked second in her high school graduating class of over 600. She was readily admitted by Omnibus University, where her grandmother rented her an off-campus apartment and provided a hefty monthly subsistence allowance. At Omnibus her freshman year, Charmaine participated in numerous extra-curricular organizations, and was one of five finalists for homecoming queen. How could life have been better?

The summer between her freshman and sophomore years in college, Charmaine enjoyed two month-long ocean cruises, to the Mediterranean and to Alaska. But back home, Grandmother Schelling's business experienced a series of devastating financial downturns and abruptly went bankrupt. The reality of losing access to her grandmother's checkbook was excruciating. How could Charmaine retain the lifestyle she enjoyed so much?

Reflecting on people she reckoned could help, one friend came to mind most often. Her hometown banker just might lend a hand – and some money. When she told him about her dilemma, the banker – a middle-aged man whose spouse's deteriorating health led him to wallow in self-pity and seek sexual reassurances outside his marriage – offered a temporary solution. Since Charmaine had neither job nor equity to offer as loan collateral, the banker proposed to make a personal loan in exchange for personal favors. The nineteen-year-old charmer accepted the proposition, and eventually got into the banker's pockets for more than forty grand.

During her sophomore year at Omnibus, Charmaine decided she should seek part-time work to still further enhance her bank account. The jobs section of the *Collegeville Daily Citizen* put her in touch with a local architectural firm. Her captivating ways readily brought results – a relatively high-paying part-time job. At Lewis & Miner, she soon caught the attention of a senior partner, who invited Charmaine to be his travel companion on trips required to transmit bids for future contracts. One thing led to another, and soon Arnie Lewis, too, was caught up in an exchange of money for sex.

Lewis & Miner provided routine consulting services to a high-ranking administrator at Omnibus University, whose responsibilities included oversight of all construction and remodeling of university facilities. Believing that Charmaine's persona could help bring additional business from Omnibus to the firm, the senior partner – who had become quite intimate with her by that time, and who over the next several months would hand her nearly thirty thousand dollars – turned to her for assistance.

Before long, this new contact at Omnibus was doing his own personal dealing with Charmaine. Within weeks, they were spending weekends together and, in exchange for his helping her land a full-time job as an apprentice financial officer in a college office, he, too, became intimate with the irresistible beauty.

By now both the banker and the architect had sunk tens of thousands of dollars in their privileged arrangements with

Charmaine Schelling. But, of course, neither wanted public disclosure of their lapses in business acumen, pecuniary wisdom, and personal morals. Their good names and reputations would surely suffer. So they "wrote off" their monetary losses as the price they had to pay for the experiences with Charmaine they had enjoyed so much.

It comes as no surprise that these extensive extracurricular activities were taking their toll on Charmaine's academic performance. She dropped out of college soon after accepting the full-time position. Her new relationship flourished until she started an intimate relationship with the person who approved travel advances in the university business office. To support her lifestyle and greed for things money can buy, Charmaine Schelling devised a scheme to supplement her income. She was doing a good job, but was underpaid, she reasoned. She rationalized that the extra money she arranged to obtain really did belong to her.

Charmaine would prepare spurious travel-cash-advance vouchers for graduate students, which she would then personally cash at the business office. Because of her conscientious hard work, commendable attitude, ability to favorably impress people, service-oriented commitment to others, and ability to learn quickly, no one questioned Charmaine's handling of the business aspects of the college.

The day of reckoning came, however, when a state auditor noticed a sharp increase in the college's travel expenditures and asked the dean for an explanation. As it turned out, Charmaine Schelling had embezzled nearly a half million dollars over a three-year period. In addition to using the money to support her exceptional lifestyle, she had bought a condominium, top-line jewelry, camera equipment, and Caribbean and European weekend getaways for herself and her best-friend-of-the-weekend. When questioned, she readily admitted to the ill-fated plan.

In this case, Omnibus University made no effort to keep the story from the media, and Charmaine Schelling was promptly brought to justice. She pleaded guilty to grand larceny, and served time in prison.

Fortunately for Omnibus, Charmaine Schelling was bonded, so the university experienced minimal monetary loss. It did, however, sustain considerable institutional embarrassment. It also used the case as justification for implementing tighter internal money-handling safeguards.

ℬ ℬ ℬ

From all appearances, professors Albert Albeniz and Hubert Newman were members in good standing of the Omnibus faculty. Both had served with distinction for three years in the armed forces, and so they both were eligible to collect substantial veterans benefits. While neither chose to pursue additional coursework, both seemed driven to cash in on the GI Bill benefits to which they were entitled. One afternoon they hatched a scheme by which they could personally benefit without having to so much as turn a tap. They would simply phantom-enroll in each other's courses, then turn in sham final grades for each other.

Albeniz and Newman proceeded with their plan, an intentional perversion of integrity in order to gain personal financial reward. And they probably could have continued this fraud for years if they had not been overgenerous when it came to assigning grades to each other. Their straight "A" grades semester after semester placed them on the President's Honor Roll! In preparing congratulatory letters for the president to sign, an alert staff member recognized the professors' names, investigated, and eventually learned of the deceit, the breaches of academic and personal integrity.

The professors admitted their misdeeds, and both asked for leniency. Not wanting to bring the embarrassment of negative publicity to the university, the administration took the common course and swept the matter under the proverbial rug. Thereby, of course, they compromised the trust of sound citizens as they winked at disgusting behavior of the sort that contributes to *dry rot in the ivory tower.*

∅ ∅ ∅

For 12 years George Lang managed The Tentacles, Omnibus University's emblematic merchandise store, in a commendable manner. His responsibilities included oversight of all licensing of Omnibus Octopi emblems to manufacturers of clothing and other merchandise and memorabilia as well as operation of the campus outlet and the university's far-flung wholesale and mail-order businesses. He had a reputation of being a happy-go-lucky, responsible person of high moral standing, a good businessperson, a hard worker.

Unbeknownst to his colleagues and overseers, though, George Lang had a serious flaw: difficulty in managing his own personal finances. Over many years, he had permitted his desire for new houses, new furnishings, new appliances, new automobiles, new recreational vehicles, new boats, and big vacation trips to overwhelm his ability to pay the bills. In negative cash flow, he experienced mounting debts, high interest rates, and late credit-card and mortgage and debt-consolidation loan payments.

To whom should he turn? Having considerable personal pride, and not wanting his relatives or friends to learn of his financial predicament, Lang concluded that his best alternative was to "borrow" money from the university's booster merchandise operations. This would be temporary, he rationalized; he would pay it back as soon as possible. Over time, Lang was able to convince himself that he was overworked and underpaid and thus really deserved this special treatment. As he became braver at "borrowing" money from the retail cash registers, and as he realized that his bills were still exceeding his income plus the "borrowed" supplement, George Lang concocted another means of gaining untaxed income. He would engage a partner, and they would sell Octopus emblematic merchandise on the side.

During a fishing trip with his bowling buddy, Roger Marsh, George learned that this good friend also had overextended himself financially. A scheme began to take shape. Since Roger owned and operated a convenience store near campus, George could sell him Octopus jackets, sweatshirts, caps, umbrellas, mugs, and the like at a "discount", thereby helping both of them resolve their financial plights. The two agreed on a scheme which – like the "borrowed" dollars from the cash registers – would be only a "temporary" proposition; just long enough for both of them to "get back on their financial feet".

It was not long before the university auditor detected that the retail sales revolving account at The Tentacles was not as large as budgeted. She plotted the income from retail sales, month-by-month, over the past three years. Sure enough, there had been a substantial downturn in receipts over the past year or so. She showed the data to the vice-president for operations, who in turn conferred with the senior vice-president for administration. After analyzing the data and thoroughly discussing the matter, they both wondered: Could someone be embezzling cash or products or both? The vice-presidents discussed the situation with the president, who assured them that he would support them in getting to the bottom of the matter.

Working closely with the director of campus security, the vice-presidents devised a sting operation, complete with cameras, sound equipment, and other devices, to determine if indeed merchandise was "walking out the back door". The investigation bore fruit in abundance. George Lang must have been stealing products and embezzling money for some time.

Now, with evidence in hand, the vice-presidents and auditor went to discuss their findings with the president. Alas, new problems came to surface. George Lang's wife had been a good friend of the president's wife since their own college days together. To complicate matters further, from time to time Lang had delivered "samples", including his-and-her matching designer jogging suits, to the president's home. The president thanked his visitors and assured them that he would discuss the case with the university's general counsel.

The university attorney concurred with the president that this was a serious matter, one that could involve an indictment and court proceedings. This, they rationalized, would result in public embarrassment to the institution as well as extensive legal fees, not to mention unproductive time and effort. They agreed that a better approach would be to show their evidence to George Lang, seek some restitution, and accept a quiet resignation. The next week, the vice-presidents meekly agreed, and it was done.

The retired George Lang, at age 54, still lives in the nicest neighborhood in Collegeville, three doors down the street from Nicholas Woolfre. Resplendent in their emblematic duds, the Langs never miss an Omnibus Octopi athletic event or a chance to host the university president and his spouse for steaks in the backyard.

ॐ ॐ ॐ

It pays to have values and be honest, although the pay may come slowly.

Chinese Proverb

For three decades, Bernie Scott faithfully served Omnibus University as director of public safety and security. His warm personality and service-oriented attitude contributed to the wide circle of contacts and friends he enjoyed both on- and off-campus.

Bernie's lifelong dream of owning a business finally took root the day he placed the high bid on an old sorority house on the west side of Collegeville. His new business – The Flower Shoppe – was appropriately named for the 8 a.m. to 6 p.m. hours the public could purchase fresh-cut and silk flowers on the first floor. The attractive store was colorfully decorated with photographs, paintings, and wall hangings representing many of the 200,000 flowers of the world. Business was good and turning a tidy profit. The success encouraged Bernie Scott to become greedy and adventurous, though, and within a year he set up another enterprise on the second and third floors.

It was the immediate, incredible success of the 7 p.m. to 7 a.m. business upstairs that enabled Bernie Scott to make accelerated mortgage payments and build a travel account to pay for trips around the world in search of more floral images and collectibles.

Each upstairs room carried the name of a flower: forget-me-not, honeysuckle, lady's slipper, passion flower, peach blossom, tiger lily, wild rose, and so on. Congenial coeds served as hostesses in these rooms, where they practiced their promiscuous deeds. Each young woman had the opportunity to choose her room's floral motif in the photographs, paintings, wall hangings, and wallpaper.

The marketing plan for the upstairs business had three legs: on-campus, emphasizing occupants of organized houses and residence halls; off-campus, focusing on personnel stationed at the nearby military base; and off-campus, for a special premium, serving the off-site passions of local businessmen and community leaders who were unwilling to risk being seen patronizing the upstairs business of The Flower Shoppe.

Many of the on-campus procurements were made by student-patrol cadets who worked for Bernie Scott in his day job. Most of them were law enforcement majors who knew it was illegal to pander. But, with the increasing cost of attending college, they found the extra money a welcome addition to their wallets.

Several of Scott's former student cadets were civilian employees at the military base who agreed – for attractive commissions – to procure potential GI customers. These pimps were also authorized to make loans, and then on payday, they served as collectors, for a handsome commission, of course.

From the start, Bernie Scott's name was proudly and widely associated with the first-floor business. For over three years, though, it was not directly linked with the upstairs business. Then rumors started flying. When administrators questioned him, Scott readily admitted his involvement. When the public found out that, rather than being an arms-length leaser of facilities, Scott was himself actively engaged in the ignoble business, he became an untenable embarrassment to the university. Having been promised there would be no criminal action, Bernie Scott quietly retired and, with his spouse, moved to the Texas Riviera.

ℒ ℒ ℒ

Staff employees of Omnibus University are generally paid deplorable wages. Yet their supervisors – and there are as many as five layers of supervisors – receive compensation on a par with the academic royalty and upper crust. Moreover, there come untaxed fringe benefits, such as smoked turkeys for favored administrators all over campus just before several holidays every year. The lowly paid employees of food services resented their much more highly paid supervisors getting the holiday turkeys, but they did not complain to university-level administrators for fear of losing their jobs. They apparently either had not heard of or did not trust the Federal Whistle Blower Protection Act.

Early in his tenure as president of Omnibus University, Dr. Burton Cromley spoke favorably and frequently of reducing administration, cutting the layers and numbers of supervisors, combining and consolidating functions where possible. His primary objective was to increase overall productivity and efficiency, to make it possible to move money from administration and other nonacademic functions to teaching, scholarship, outreach, and library services, where it was urgently needed. He also wanted to increase salaries and wages of meritorious faculty and staff members.

Unfortunately, Omnibus was afflicted with the "good-ol'-boys" syndrome and saturated with strong acceptance of a culture founded on nepotism. Moreover, the dynamics of change were being crushed and suppressed at every opportunity, on every front.

When a food-service employee about to retire went to president Cromley and wept as she revealed how staff persons struggled to make personal ends meet while supervisors received special treatment in the form of food to take home, she was assured the matter would be looked into. The president asked the senior vice-president for administration and the director of security to investigate the matter.

Sure enough, supervisors were receiving special favors in the form of food. When it was called to their attention, they thought nothing of it. "It's always been done this way," they said. That practice was stopped immediately. The president expanded the investigative team, and charged it to look for other possible irregularities in the system.

Meanwhile, president Cromley had learned that there was apparent duplication of services between the physical plant division and the maintenance and housekeeping department of the residence halls division. This even meant keeping two inventories and operating two warehouses for generally the same supplies. But the president's suggestion that the inventories, warehouses, and management operations be merged into a single, more-efficient operation was met by vigorous opposition. High-ranking supervisors and campus administrators expressed strong arguments against such a move. "What you are asking for would adversely affect the quality of services to students living in the halls," they insisted.

To help block the merger, students were called upon to join the entrenched culture's campaign for *status quo*. But just as the students knew nothing about their room-and-board money being used to purchase smoked turkeys for administrators and supervisors, they also had no inkling of what was going on behind the scenes with the separate warehouse arrangement for cleaning supplies and the like. The student newspaper unmercifully lashed out at the president for being so insolent as to entertain any thought of consolidating physical-plant and residence-hall cleaning services and supply warehousing. Of course, the students were being manipulated, but they were too naive and flattered to consider such a possibility when it was called to their attention.

The easy thing for the president to do would have been to back off. Instead, true to his commitment to bring about greater efficiency, president Cromley employed a highly recommended, independent consultant to review the situation. After several days of study and confidential interviews, the outside expert recommended, among other things, merger of the two operations.

Student leaders and their daily newspaper criticized the plan bitterly, with stinging articles and distasteful cartoons that went on for weeks. But the president stayed the course and combined the functions under the auspices of the physical plant, with the understanding that the services rendered to students must improve and that overall costs must decrease.

Here is the rest of the story. The consultant had revealed that the per-student cost of supplies (cleaning agents, paper products, and other expendables) was nearly four times greater in some residence halls than in others. The president ordered that a sting operation be planned and implemented under the supervision of the director of security. Hidden cameras were installed in the warehouse to determine if cleaning supplies and products were being pilfered, and if so, by whom.

Around 3:00 a.m. every weekday, a nondescript delivery van was loaded with supplies and products that had been pur-chased with public monies. Its destination: the state's private nursing homes. By unknowingly using stolen property fraudulently sold to them at a discount, nursing home operators could cut costs and increase profits. Of course, crooked university employees were engaged in a highly profitable side business.

So what was done? As with much *dry rot in the ivory tower*, and against president Cromley's better judgment, virtu-ally nothing. A couple of the employees most directly involved resigned. But once again the felonious acts were swept under the rug. Why? To avoid embarrassment to the institution and to protect the professional careers of certain high administrators in Omnibus University who had for years been letting their oversight skimmers leak.

> Quite as important as legislation is vigilant oversight of administration.
> **Woodrow Wilson (1856-1924)**
> **Twenty-eighth President, United States of America**

⚥ ⚥ ⚥

Hugo Sherbane was president of Omnibus University Foundation, an autonomous corporation that serves as the university's principal private fund-raising organization. His first appearance suggested a friendly, well-groomed gentleman. But people soon discovered that he was an insecure person with extravagant tastes and a terminal case of egocentrism.

University president Burton Cromley knew that Sherbane had been passed over for promotion several times in the corporate world. Top officers of the last company Sherbane worked for were pleased when his friends at Omnibus orchestrated his appointment to the helm of his alma mater's foundation.

From the outset, president Cromley had serious philosophical differences with Sherbane. To whom did the private monies donated to the foundation belong? Sherbane thought they were his own to manage and spend as he pleased. Cromley believed instead that they had been donated to the university and were simply parked temporarily in the foundation's coffers.

Soon after taking charge, Sherbane committed substantial funds to remodeling the foundation's headquarters, all without consulting even one member of the foundation board, let alone anyone else.

Further, the foundation head autocratically decided to subsidize the local chamber of commerce by paying chamber membership dues for dozens of foundation and university employees, a handful of university retirees, and a few personal friends. The president believed the university community should support the local chamber, but that membership dues should not be paid from foundation funds, which had been donated and were intended for library acquisitions, scholarships, and other high-priority needs.

A third example of Hugo Sherbane's spending foundation money as if it were his own surfaced when he privately negotiated with a music professor to sponsor a program using undergraduate student talent and university instruments and equipment. Conferring with no one, he agreed to pay the faculty member thousands of dollars annually to sponsor and coordinate the group. This pegged that faculty member's total income far above the norm, resulting in morale problems in the music school.

President Cromley also believed that Sherbane was not raising enough private money. Omnibus ranked last among its peer institutions in total endowment as well as annual private giving, and there was no strategic plan to change rank. The foundation was unique among its peers in that it had never conducted a comprehensive private fund-raising campaign. When concerns were raised, however, Sherbane sarcastically reminded Cromley that the president did not hold membership on the foundation's governing board.

Another issue standing in the way of a productive working relationship between Cromley and Sherbane was how the foundation president squandered money – dollars donors had given, believing they would go to further the best interests of the university. When traveling with Sherbane, university personnel traveled business class, rented expensive vehicles, patronized first-class hotels and four-star restaurants. At mealtime, Sherbane himself commonly ordered wine, costing as much as $80 a bottle, even when dining alone.

Once, when the Sherbanes were scheduled to host a party in their home, he was reminded that they needed a new tablecloth. Without hesitating, he scheduled a trip with Mrs. Sherbane to a distant city and contracted with Omnibus flight services to provide the chartered transportation, which cost more than twice what commercial flights would have. The official purpose of that tablecloth-motivated overnight shopping spree, which included an elegant dinner and drinks at an exclusive supper club and lodging at a five-star hotel for the Sherbanes and their pilots, was "donor grooming". The excursion cost the foundation over $3500 – hardly a prudent expenditure of money contributed by donors who believed their gifts would be used to fund undergraduate scholarships and other high-priority programs at Omnibus.

Several foundation employees shared with university officials examples of serious wastes of foundation money and how
Sherbane's falsification of records caused problems. Two resigned on principle. Having a well-paid, prestigious white-collar
job weighed heavily on the minds of others, who would have
preferred to resign but, having no equivalent job opportunity
elsewhere, elected to stay put.

When the foundation purchased a full-sized automobile for
Sherbane's use, he worked out a deal with the dealer that called
for the foundation to pay full sticker price for the new car. The
dealer in turn subtracted several thousand dollars – the ordinary
discount on an expensive car sold to a non-profit organization –
from the purchase price of a less expensive automobile
purchased privately for Mrs. Sherbane's use.

Hugo Sherbane had a cozy way of selecting members of the
foundation board, too. He enjoyed taking cruises – as many as
five a year – on which he would host, at foundation expense,
prospective members of the foundation's governing board. Then,
if all went well, he would orchestrate bringing them on as
members of the board. Having steadfast board members was
critical to Sherbane's job security when, for example, an
investigative reporter learned from a concerned former
foundation employee that, while building a pretentious new
house, Sherbane used foundation funds to install a stereo system
costing more than $37,000 "for use in hosting prospective
donors". And in preparing to secure a very low-interest personal
loan to build his ostentatious house, it was convenient that
Sherbane selected a new board member who was the chief loan
officer of the local bank to which he earlier had redirected the
foundation's banking business without bid competition.

The personal pleasure Hugo Sherbane derived from travel
surfaced again when an alumnus, then residing in Bermuda, arrived on campus with check in hand to establish another perma-
nently endowed President's Scholar. Sherbane quickly saw this
as a way to get an expense-paid trip to the Caribbean for him

and his spouse – and to return with a check to show how profitable the trip had proved to be. So he told the donor that he needed to do some paperwork related to the scholarship endowment and, further, he would soon be coming to Bermuda anyway, and they could finalize the gift at that time.

Foundation employees told president Cromley, too, about the snow jobs Sherbane routinely gave the foundation board on financial matters. He would present a proposed budget, but then, if income had been short or expenses long that year, he would revise the data when presenting the budget-year-in-review to his board the next time around.

When a major donor accused Sherbane of mismanaging foundation funds, employed the services of an out-of-town attorney, and called for an in-depth investigation and comprehensive audit, foundation employees advised president Cromley that records were falsified and travel and expense vouchers constructed and reconstructed – and signed by former chairs of the foundation's governing board for whom Sherbane held chits. A massive effort was launched within the foundation to cover Sherbane's tracks and leave no questionable paper trail. In some cases, weekends were spent purging files as deemed necessary as the audit date drew near. By the time the state audit team arrived, the files were in order.

Besides, when it was learned that Hugo Sherbane had contributed hundreds of dollars to the reelection campaigns of the state auditor as well as the governor, few people expected much would be found wrong. When the auditor was given a heads-up, he failed to follow through in discussing irregularities with former employees who had agreed to share pertinent information. Sherbane had convinced the auditor that these people simply had personal axes to grind.

Finally, encouraged to take early retirement and provide the foundation the opportunity to erase question marks related to his management, Hugo Sherbane negotiated a lucrative separation package that included hefty one-time payments, annuities, a major insurance package, and other expensive perquisites.

But all these goodies were not enough for Sherbane, who wanted to select his own replacement to boot. So he employed the services of a private firm specializing in executive searches. He manipulated the process so as to make certain that two highly qualified candidates would not reach the short list. Both happened to be people who saw through Sherbane's facade.

To ensure that his hand-picked replacement would receive the support of the foundation executive committee, Hugo Sherbane unilaterally appointed two additional members to that body the week the final interviews were to be conducted. Happy and confident, he staged a celebratory party for the executive committee and other selected friends at his home the night before the hiring-decision vote was to be taken. His heir-apparent was on hand so he could conveniently visit with a hand-picked real estate agent about houses.

But the following day, when president Burton Cromley was asked – almost as an afterthought – by the chair of the foundation's executive committee if the favored candidate would be acceptable to the university family, Cromley was ready. He cited results of feedback he had from vice-presidents, deans, alumni leaders, and others, all of whom virtually unanimously had said "no". Hugo Sherbane's choice was not appointed.

> It is impossible to escape the impression that people commonly use false standards of measurement – they seek power, success, and wealth for themselves and admire them in others, and they underestimate what is of true value in life.
> **Sigmund Freud (1856-1939)**
> **Austrian psychiatrist**

> Because power corrupts, society's demands for moral authority and character increase as the importance of the position increases.
> **John Adams (1735-1826)**
> **Second President, United States of America**

REMEMBERING ... *The Tales of Two Students*

Unless higher education shifts course and does so soon, some institutions will be swept aside by the tidal wave of the information revolution and its harbingers, the commercial providers of education eager to provide employers and students with education "packages" tailored to what these "customers" think they need.

Robert H. Atwell, President Emeritus,
American Council on Education (1996)

Any increase in tuition limits access, and the impact is differentially hurtful for the economically disadvantaged, minorities, and recent immigrant groups.

James B. Appleberry, President, American Association of State
Colleges and Universities, cited by Jean Evangelauf, "Tuition Rises
Again," *The Chronicle of Higher Education*, **October 5, 1994, p. A41**

Access to quality higher education is one of the proudest traditions New Yorkers have. But ... sentimentality is not at work here. An educated work force is surely as crucial to the city's and state's economic health as lower taxes, the goals to which higher education is being sacrificed ... . Cutting off their access is not only unjust ... it is economically self-defeating.

"Destructive Tuition Hikes" (editorial),
New York Times, **March 17, 1995, p. E31**

Regular readers of AAF will recall my abiding concern with higher education's profound lack of accountability; a lack of accountability which is the root cause of a pattern of self-serving behavior which has in turn led to its inefficiencies – not the least of which are immense costs of a system more concerned with resisting substantive change than embracing it.

Robert W. Tucker, Founder and Editor, *Adult Assessment Forum*
Journal of Quality Management in Adult-Centered Education
Winter 1997, Vol. VII (4), p. 3

Many administrators say that while the most sought-after applicants are prospering, many good but not spectacular students with a need for financial help, including those in minorities, are less able to get it. The role that colleges had taken on in the 1960s to make the best education available to all sectors in society is being compromised.

Ethan Bronner, *The New York Times*, **June 21, 1998, pp. 1,18**

CHAPTER 8

ATHLETICS: BUSINESS AS USUAL

> Does college pay? It does if you are a good open-field runner!
>> **Will Rogers (1879-1935)**
>> **American humorist and author**

> Things which matter most must never be at the mercy of things which matter least.
>> **Johann Wolfgang von Goethe (1749-1832)**
>> **German poet**

Jason Gates was a standout running back at Rivonia High School. Although slight in physical stature, he was a conscientious, determined, hard-working athlete with a can-do attitude. Jason was devoted to his mother, a woman of high values, great patience, and marvelous disposition. She worked as a hospital nurse's aide, took health-care-related coursework at night school, and served as a model mother for a large family. She loved her children and made each of them feel special.

To attend college, Jason Gates would need financial aid. A football scholarship seemed to be a wise first try. Jason greatly impressed his high school coach, and his teammates and other classmates alike admired and respected him. When praised for his athletic feats, Jason would give his teammates more than their fair share of credit for his own success.

His high school football coach sent video tapes showcasing the star athlete's skills as a running back to NCAA Division I institutions in which the young man had expressed interest. But none of them expressed interest in Jason Gates. The head coach of one major collegiate football program even told Jason's coach that the last thing he needed was a midget, that he already knew of 100 walk-ons, and if Jason Gates wanted to be number 101, "he can be my guest". Jason and his family and a large group of supporters were disappointed. They had dreamed of his playing on a nationally-ranked team.

After being turned down by the first half-dozen schools of his choice, Jason Gates accepted a scholarship to attend Omnibus University, a Division I institution whose football program, in recent years, had shown promise of better days ahead.

Jason was warmly received by fellow players when he arrived at Omnibus for football practice. They admired his athletic abilities, appreciated his attitude, and noticed his humility and sincerity. Jason quickly assumed a prominent place in the Fellowship of Christian Athletes on campus. He also was a conscientious student in a demanding academic major – business management, attending classes regularly, studying hard, and making good grades.

Early on, the coaches recognized that Jason Gates could be an impact player and bring a new level of excitement to the Octopus football program. He disappointed no one. His freshman year, Jason ran behind a football great who was a finalist to win the Heisman Trophy and who went on to star with a prominent National Football League team. He ran strong his sophomore year, too, and was touted as a potential All-American player his junior year. Indeed, that year he set new conference and NCAA rushing records before being selected as the nation's best intercollegiate football player and winner of the coveted Heisman Trophy.

Throughout that junior season – major bowl game included, where again he set rushing and scoring records – Jason Gates maintained his modesty, giving credit for his running success to the offensive linemen who consistently blocked and tackled to open the trail he would blaze. Never did he claim personal credit for his accomplishments. He really did not want to be selected as the Heisman Trophy winner, believing that any team's success is a team effort, that no one individual should be so honored.

Nevertheless, he received tremendously favorable media coverage. Alumni groups and school assemblies, among others, invited Jason Gates to visit and offer remarks. He honored as many requests as he could, not because he craved attention, but because he saw opportunities to witness for his God and his country and to share his experiences in "just saying no" to alcohol, drugs, and tobacco. Jason Gates served as a superb role model for people of all ages.

> The first great gift we can bestow on others is a good example.
>
> **Thomas Morell**

> Once there was a man whose neighbors held him to be a great man ... . We know he is a great man, they said, "because when we are with him we ourselves feel bigger".
>
> **James M. Spinning (1892-1973)**

For personal reasons, Jason Gates elected to make himself available to the National Football League draft following his junior year in college. He signed an attractive contract that included a hefty signing bonus. Then he promptly gave 10 percent of that bonus to his hometown church, and has gone on to assist members of his family with business arrangements, to support his siblings in attending college, plus other demonstrations of his generosity and humility.

Jason Gates is a great credit to his family, to the community of faith, and to this nation's program of intercollegiate athletics.

ဆ ဆ ဆ

With strong support and encouragement from Omnibus alumni and trustees, the president (and trustee Malcomb Russell) selected Jeremy Bateman to serve as Omnibus athletics director. Bateman had been a two-time All-American basketball guard for the Octopi a decade earlier. He played professional basketball six years before an injury forced early retirement. Meanwhile, he returned to Collegeville, where he entered into a partnership with friends in an insurance agency and with relatives in an interior decorating business.

Jeremy Bateman was extremely popular with alumni and friends of Omnibus. He had it all. He had brought national recognition to Omnibus as a collegian when the team participated in back-to-back NCAA Final Four competitions. He had been a successful player in the National Basketball Association. And he was a successful businessperson, a truly nice guy. Most of all, "he's one of our own", alumni would say. And when trustee Sallie Snell-Schumacher said it, it was with an indescribable look of pride and joy on her face.

The new AD immediately was facing a major fiscal challenge. The athletics department had been operating in the red for more than a decade. Each year, when informed of the budgetary shortfall, the governing board would make it short shrift and simply tell the president, "Fix it!" That the president had done, year after year. But there had been costs: reduced library acquisitions, closed sections of large-enrollment required courses, deferred campus computerization and classroom maintenance, and a shortage of money to initiate and fund new and ongoing high-priority educational programs, to mention a few.

Without discussing the alternatives and his overall fiscal strategies with the president, the popular Jeremy Bateman became creative. He began trading out tickets to football and basketball games – the two most reliable income-generating sports – to local motels, restaurants, and other businesses, in exchange for rooms, meals, dry cleaning, and other services that would spare the expenditure side of the athletics operation's ledger. Of course, it decreased the revenue side, as well. All of this was done with virtually no record or accountability, eventually creating a nightmare for Omnibus and state auditors.

Concurrently, Bateman gave all of the athletics department's insurance and decorating business to the companies of which he was still part-owner. Few questioned his practice of giving the department's substantial concessions business to close friends. Some, he would say, were potential donors, and all were reliable and appreciative of the trade. But when he signed a $12,000 contract with his interior decorating business without going through the state-mandated bid process, a competitor squawked in a letter of complaint published in the *Collegeville Daily Citizen*. This step of Bateman's was perceived by many as a step too far. Several prominent members of the public communicated their feelings to the president.

In discussing the matter with the trustees, president Fred Finnigan deduced that Jeremy Bateman was a close personal friend of several board members, and that they had accepted favors and special privileges from him. In short, the trustees supported Jeremy Bateman. In fact, so long as reports of questionable practices at Omnibus were kept out of the state and national media, the board was completely tolerant of what many in the know perceived as questionable judgments. "After all, he's one of our own," added trustee Sallie Snell-Schumacher.

> In several cases, board members have declined to support the efforts of presidents to clean up their athletic programs, but rather have aligned themselves with popular coaches, athletic directors, or booster groups – in effect, declaring by their actions (or lack of them) that athletics are more important than academics or integrity.
> **John B. Slaughter (b. 1934)**
> **Former Chancellor, University of Maryland**
> **President, Occidental College**

𝄞 𝄞 𝄞

Karl Karbo had been a football star at Omnibus University, a player who truly made a difference in the win:loss tallies, game attendance, and football excitement during his years wearing the Octopus purple and black. Through an agent, Karbo signed a lucrative multiple-year contract with a competitive National Football League team. The agreement included a hefty signing bonus that enabled him to purchase an expensive automobile and a new house for his mother as well as, unfortunately, underwrite the pleasure he derived from using recreational drugs.

After four successful seasons of professional football – during which he earned exorbitant salaries and tested positive for drugs on three occasions – his periods of probation for drug abuse ran out, and he found himself unemployed, financially broke, but still chemically dependent. His appeal for one more probationary opportunity was an emotional plea which included his admitting that, even though he "graduated" from Omnibus University, he could neither read nor write. Moreover, Karl Karbo revealed that others who wanted to be helpful had done his homework, taken examinations for him, and helped him remain academically eligible to play.

This was news not only for the sports pages. It resulted in stories in the national mass media about this professional football player who had been abused by Omnibus University – kept eligible to play football by terrible instances of academic course scheduling, unauthorized academic assistance, and the like.

The case generated, in equal measures, public sentiment in support of drug-addict Karl Karbo and resentment among the general alumni of Omnibus University. The alumni sent telegrams, made telephone calls, and mailed letters of disgust to the president and others.

Anyway, his strategy worked, and Karl Karbo was given "one more" opportunity to play professional football, with the provision that he participate in a drug-rehabilitation program.

Meanwhile, the Omnibus administration was busy studying the case and responding to the heat generated by the matter. Some people said they had destroyed their Omnibus diplomas, they were so angry, ashamed, and embarrassed. A thorough and unbiased review of Karbo's academic record revealed that, even though he had spent four years of intercollegiate football eligibility, he was more than 50 semester hours short of completing requirements for a baccalaureate degree. And, in fact, he had not received a diploma. Clearly, the institution had erred in permitting the manipulation and abuse of courses scheduled to maintain Karl Karbo's athletic eligibility.

> The university's worth must be measured in terms of impact on both the individual and society. The university must lead the way in our search for a better society; it must be an instrument for both change and continuity as we seek truth, beauty, goodness and justice.
>
> **Gladys S. Johnston**

The damage had been done through inaccurate media reporting that Karl Karbo had been awarded a bachelor's degree by Omnibus University even though he could neither read nor write. Nevertheless, the new president appointed a blue-ribbon committee comprised primarily of respected senior faculty members, and charged them to offer recommendations to safeguard against such abuse of academic programs in the future.

The tremendous outcry of alumni notwithstanding, two Omnibus trustees told the president that it had been worth the temporary bad publicity. From board member Cutter Humphery's perspective, Karl Karbo alone had virtually turned the Octopus football program around. He had generated a high level of excitement as the win:loss record reversed, attendance at home and away games significantly increased, and – after a twenty-year hiatus – Omnibus University was invited to participate in a major bowl game two years in a row.

✍ ✍ ✍

When J. Newton Gresham was hired as Omnibus director of athletics, he expected to raise the large sums of private money needed to expand and repair the football stadium, construct new dressing rooms and physical fitness facilities, build a new baseball field, and recruit a football coach who would quickly turn that program around. Gresham's positive attitude and persuasive personality helped accomplish these things and more in just four years.

Gresham recruited as head football coach Wilcomb Washburn, a former football great at Omnibus who later played in the National Football League for seven years before joining the coaching staff of a Super Bowl champion team. His reputation and charm, coupled with modernized facilities, enabled Washburn to recruit outstanding junior-college transfer students who gave virtually instant success to the Octopus football program. An invitation to a major bowl game came already his second season at the helm, and again his third and fourth years. The alumni were becoming excited. Private contributions to the athletics program doubled and redoubled before increasing to ten times the pre-Gresham rate in both the fourth and fifth years.

The new baseball field helped rejuvenate that program, too, and by the fourth year of Gresham's tenure, the Omnibus baseball team had earned a berth in the NCAA College World Series. But at those games in Omaha, the first in a series of developments occurred that spelled trouble for the popular, highly successful director of athletics.

A large following of Omnibus University baseball fans made the long trek to Omaha without tickets. There simply were not enough tickets allotted to Omnibus to satisfy the demand. Based on previous experiences, these collegiate baseball enthusiasts believed they would be able to buy tickets at the box office in Omaha. The shocker came when they bought the tickets in Omaha, all right, but had to purchase them "through the fence" from members of Gresham's own staff.

This scheme triggered high suspicion: Who was benefiting from these unauthorized sales? And following the College World Series – in which the Octopi nine played in the finals – the disgruntled, concerned Purple and Black fans called and wrote the president of their alma mater regarding the practice of staff members' selling tickets at inflated prices for cash. Gresham denied having any knowledge of the unauthorized ticket sales, but promised to look into the matter.

Soon thereafter, an embittered employee in the physical plant tipped off a *Collegeville Daily Citizen* reporter that J. Newton Gresham had engaged the university's physical plant to remodel the kitchen, recreation room, and garage of his private home. The headline article brought outcries of abuse of privileges by local alumni and taxpayers. Again, calls and letters poured into the president's office.

The president launched an investigation, which confirmed that director J. Newton Gresham had used athletics department funds to pay for cabinets, lumber, paint, and other supplies as well as labor to employ the services of the Omnibus physical plant to remodel his kitchen cabinets, build trophy cases in his recreation room, and construct new shelves and storage facilities in his garage. Gresham also had traded tickets to sporting events for laundry and dry cleaning services for himself and his family. Other tickets had been traded for dining at expensive local and capital-city restaurants by family and friends. And to add insult to injury, the clothes cleaning business and restaurant had, for tax purposes, been given credit for contributions to Omnibus University in amounts equal to the personal services rendered to Gresham and his clan.

Because of Gresham's high profile, these incidents were picked up by the national media, and considerable public pressure was brought to bear on the president to fire him. Interestingly, alumni were divided on the matter. As many noted, Gresham had brought a new era – a new level of enthusiasm and private giving – to athletics at Omnibus, and if he would demonstrate remorse and make restitution for his wrongful acts, they would be willing to see him given a second chance. Other alumni felt just as strongly that, in light of what had happened, they could no longer trust Gresham and would contribute nothing more to the Octopus cause as long as he was in charge. Fortunately, with all the adverse publicity for Omnibus – plus

the personal stress and anxiety – Gresham himself soon elected
to resign.

> I am easily satisfied with the very best.
> **Sir Winston Churchill (1874-1965)**
> **Prime Minister, United Kingdom**
> **(1940-1945; 1951-1955)**

🔊 🔊 🔊

Length of service guaranteed, salary level assured, and
other provisions of contracts enjoyed by most collegiate
Division I athletic coaches primarily reflect win:loss records,
placing enormous pressure on coaches to win. Their job is to
identify and recruit the best raw talent, keep athletes
academically eligible, and coach to win. Herm Scholofsky, head
football coach at Omnibus University for a time, through his
ambitious and creative academic counselor, maintained a full
roster of eligible athletes.

With connections both on-campus and off-, Oscar Osgood
was confident in academic matters. He worked to remain favorably viewed by faculty members who – for a few good tickets and
the opportunity to travel with the team to away games – would
"fix" grades. Moreover, these were the sort of flexible
professors who, if their courses did not fulfill the curricular
needs of student-athletes, had experienced graduate students
from other institutions in the state who – in exchange for another
round of perks – in turn had *their* connections, and could arrange
courses at *their* institutions for credit-transfer purposes.

The year he was told that seven starters needed summer
credits to be eligible to play that fall presented a special
challenge, even for academic counselor par excellence Oscar
Osgood. Two had been All-Conference stars the previous
season, one an All-American candidate. The courses offered by
Osgood's most reliable on-campus connections would not satisfy
the NCAA rule requiring "satisfactory academic progress". So
he turned for help to his off-campus network.

And did he ever get help! He arranged to have cash paid for the tuition, fees, and expenses incurred to enroll all seven athletes in a bogus economics course at Culver State University, on the other side of the state.

His connection at Culver State, in turn, had a connection in the registrar's office who had access to the CSU official seal stamp. So without actually matriculating, without showing up for a single class meeting, without taking a single examination, indeed without ever setting foot on the Culver State University campus, all seven athletes enrolled in the phantom course, and all received a final grade of "B", sufficient in each case to assure continuing eligibility. The money ostensibly paid for tuition and fees, books, and the official institutional transcript reflecting college credit for an absolutely bogus economics course was divided among the graduate student from the credit-granting institution (an advisee of Oscar Osgood's Omnibus faculty connection); the Culver State instructor of the sham economics course, who assigned the grades; and the staff employee in the Culver State University Office of Registrar, who affixed the official seal of that institution to the transcripts.

The motto of many academic administrators ... is the motto of careerists everywhere – "No trouble on my watch." There is all too frequently more interest in avoiding high-profile problems than in achieving academic and intellectual greatness.

From *The Shadow University:*
The Betrayal of Liberty on America's Campuses
by **Alan C. Kors** and **Harvey A. Silverglate**
Copyright © 1998 by Harvey A. Silverglate and Alan C. Kors
Reprinted with permission of The Free Press,
a Division of Simon & Schuster, Inc.

Sports ought to provide a spiritual catharsis, which cannot occur if participants are overly dedicated to winning, or if spectators allow their partisanship to get out of hand.
James A. Michener (1907-1997)
American author

REMEMBERING ... *The Tales of Two Students*

Some middle-class families insist that they are the ones being locked out of the best possible higher education. They say they are victims of a "middle class squeeze," in which rich families can afford tuition no matter how fast it rises, and poor families are given substantial grants and subsidized loans. The middle class, meanwhile, faces ever more-surreal tuition bills without help.

Stephen Burd, Patrick Healy, Kit Lively, and Christopher Shea
"Low-Income Students Say Their College Options Are Limited"
The Chronicle of Higher Education, **June 14, 1996, p. A12**

Economists worry about the accelerating bifurcation in the wage and class structure – the income and opportunity differential between the well-educated and the poorly educated .... The lack of education will virtually condemn a worker to a path that has been declining in real wages and thus has been growing ever-distant from the wages of the educated.

Robert W. Tucker
Adult Assessment Forum, **Spring 1995, p. 3**

A pattern of decreased enrollments at our public universities that traditionally provide the best education at the least cost should be viewed as a warning flag. It signals that rising tuition costs and the availability of fewer need-based grants may be causing serious financial hardship to some qualified students and denying them access and opportunity.

C. Peter Magrath, President
National Association of State Universities and Land-Grant Colleges
NASULGC Newsline, **October 1994, p. 4**

Rising college tuitions are real. In the 20 years between 1976 and 1996, the average tuition at public universities increased from $642 to $3151 (391%) and the average tuition at private universities increased from $2881 to $15,581 (441%). Tuition at public two-year colleges, the least expensive of all types of institutions, increased from an average of $245 to $1245 (408%) during this period.

"Straight Talk About College Costs and Prices"
January 1998 report of the 11-member National Commission
appointed by the US Congress in accordance with
Public Law 105-18 (Title IV, Cost of Higher Education Review, 1997)

CHAPTER 9

STUDENTS: UH-H-H ... OH YEAH!

> Could I climb to the highest place in Athens, I
> would lift my voice and proclaim, "Fellow citizens,
> why do you turn and scrape every stone to gather
> wealth and take so little care of your children to
> whom one day you must relinquish it all?"
>
> **Socrates (470-399 BC)**
> **Greek philosopher**

> Individuals, like flowers that are not watered
> regularly, wither and die. When we abandon people
> and their hopes and dreams, we encourage them to
> become mediocre. People seek and need positive re-
> inforcement.
>
> **Christine Licata**

Donald Franklin was the youngest of the nine children raised by Carolyn Franklin, a compassionate woman who dropped out of high school to enter motherhood as a single parent at age fifteen. The Franklin family grew up in a tough neighborhood of a large city, where crime and poverty prevailed, and where being inducted into the local gang was the surest way to find a means of making money – mostly pushing and pimping. None of Donald's blood relatives had continued their education beyond high school. Most, in fact, dropped out, unprepared to break out of the rut in which many inner-city residents find themselves.

Donald's mother hoped that one of her sons would play professional sports, so he could rescue the family, but it had not happened. And she prayed that some of her children would excel in school, then prepare for a better life through a college education. She knew that Donald had above-average academic abilities, but she also knew that his schooling was deficient. She was unable to help him at all in his favorite subjects – science and mathematics. Moreover, even if he were admitted, how could he afford a college education?

Fortunately, as it turned out, through a special private grant-in-aid program for the financially disadvantaged, Donald Franklin received a scholarship to study engineering at Omnibus University. Two substantial part-time jobs rounded out the financial-aid package he needed in order to be able to pursue what had gradually become his goal.

Well-prepared in neither middle school nor high school for competing in a demanding curriculum, and pressed by the time demands of his two extracurricular jobs, Donald was over-whelmed by the academic rigors of college. He failed to perform satisfactorily his first semester, and was placed on scholastic probation. His grades were no better the second semester so, following academic rules at Omnibus University, he was suspended.

Donald Franklin had made many friends his freshman year. The family of one of them owned a bridge-construction company and offered Donald summer employment. He quickly accepted. But now how was he going to tell his classmate that he would not be returning to college in the fall?

Donald was proud to share with his mother the exciting news about the summer job. But when he told her of his academic suspension, Carolyn Franklin was heartbroken. She badgered him about the reasons. Would he study harder next time? Was he determined to succeed if given another opportunity? Donald told his mother that he believed, if given a third chance, he would be a successful student.

Having neither a telephone at home nor the cash to place a toll call at a public phone, Carolyn Franklin went to the office at Donald's high school and asked if she could use the telephone there to call the dean of engineering at Omnibus. Reluctantly, the receptionist gave her permission.

Upon reaching Dr. Harold Twinning, associate dean for academic programs in engineering, Carolyn Franklin arranged for an appointment to discuss Donald's case the following week.

The intervening days seemed an eternity for the heartsick but determined mother. She took a clock her own mother had been given for caring for a terminally ill neighbor many years earlier to a neighborhood pawn shop to obtain the money needed to buy the ticket for the bus trip.

In dean Twinning's office, although she was unnerved by the unfamiliar place, Carolyn Franklin got down to basics in a heartbeat. She briefly reviewed the family history, the lack of financial resources, relating how she had purchased Donald's college clothes at a Salvation Army thrift store.

Most importantly, Carolyn Franklin told the dean that if Donald were not permitted to try again, he would return home at the end of the summer, to be met by the local gang leaders. They would give him two choices: become a partner in their drug and flesh enterprises or be found in a back-alley dumpster. "They're waiting for him," she assured the dean. Weeping, she begged dean Twinning to make an exception and grant Donald a third try.

After asking the devoted mother a few questions about her son's commitment to improving his academic performance, Harold Twinning asked to take a break. For five minutes, he stood staring out his window, his mind racing. He was aware of the policy requiring him to seek faculty counsel in such matters. But he had heard enough. He had been touched by this driven woman's plea. He granted her request on the spot.

> When in doubt, do what is right.
> **Mark Twain (1835-1910)**
> **American writer**

Dean Twinning is frequently heard to say that nothing, in the course of his more than three decades in college work, has given him more satisfaction than knowing he had helped make it possible to see Donald Franklin's proud mother sitting on a front-row seat at graduation ceremonies, beaming and with tears running down her cheeks as she celebrated her son's earning an Omnibus University engineering degree.

Donald Franklin was pleased, too. Pleased that he had prepared himself for a career that would enable him to repay his caring mother, who had gone to the mat for him so he could break out of the ghetto, her due.

ℒ ℒ ℒ

Dr. Gilbert Garrett, a full professor of economics at Omnibus, was utterly dedicated to the education of all students, regardless of family, economic, or cultural background. He was a regular volunteer in the institution's Office of High School and College Relations that offered Omnibus Night programs all over the state.

At one of these events, all through his brief remarks, in which he encouraged the students to "never give up" and to continue their education, Dr. Garrett's eyes returned several times to a young woman seated in a back corner of the room. She appeared to be a shy, self-effacive person.

After the program, Brenda Upcreek waited until everyone else had left the auditorium to ask Dr. Garrett if he thought she could succeed at Omnibus. Without knowing her high school grades, pre-college test scores, or degree of motivation, Garrett responded that, if she was determined and willing to study hard and make certain sacrifices, indeed she could.

Brenda's face flushed as she admitted that she knew nothing about things like applying for admission, part-time work, financial aid. But if he were willing to help, she sincerely wanted to pursue a college education. This people-oriented professor saw something in Brenda's eyes that clinched it for him. He would do all he could to help her attain her goals.

What we have done for ourselves alone dies with us.
What we have done for others and the world remains and is
immortal.
Albert Pine

Garrett proceeded. When Brenda learned there would be a
$20 application fee, she became emotional and said she would
need to think some more about this. She would not tell Garrett
that she would receive neither encouragement nor financial help
from her parents or that she did not have and was unlikely to
have the spare $20. Sensing the problem, however, Garrett
quickly added that the application fee should not be a hurdle (he
would quietly provide the $20 himself).

Although Brenda wished to enroll in the College of Education, which was not Garrett's college home, he helped her enroll,
obtain a part-time job in the library, and complete the paperwork
needed to apply for financial aid. He served as Brenda's
unofficial faculty adviser all through her four years of college.

You simply give to others a bit of yourself – a
thoughtful act, a helpful idea, a world of appreciation, a lift
over a rough spot, a sense of understanding, a timely suggestion.
Charles H. Burr

During her first semester at Omnibus, Brenda Upcreek
found the courage to share with professor Garrett facts that made
him all the more glad that he had encouraged her to go to
college. Brenda had been an abused child. Both of her parents
were alcoholics. Her mother would shake and abuse her
verbally, and Brenda never knew whether or not she would be
invited to the dinner table. Her father would belt and curse her
so much that often she would leave the house by the front door
as he entered by the back door. Many nights she slept with her
dog on a blanket on the garage floor or, on hot summer nights,
along the backyard fence.

What effects, Garrett wondered, had such a family environment had on Brenda's high school grades, her aptitude test

scores, her overall state-of-being? Of one thing he was confident: The encouragement of a caring friend and attainment of additional education were critical to Brenda's self-esteem and future ability to contribute to society. College admission policies, he concluded, should include provisions for such students – policies that are more inclusive.

> They teach me to do good when they do me good.
> **Thomas Fuller (1608-1661)**
> **English author**

Brenda Upcreek graduated with a bachelor's degree in elementary education, and today she is a caring second-grade teacher. She also is a regular volunteer with local agencies working with abused children.

> This nation's greatest strength is not its weapons, but its people. Our greatest hope is not technology, but the potential of coming generations. Education is, as it has always been, an investment in the future of the nation.
> **Ernest L. Boyer (1929-1995)**
> **President, Carnegie Foundation for the**
> **Advancement of Teaching (1980-1995)**

ॐ ॐ ॐ

Jacqueline Johnson was a people-oriented full professor of biology at Omnibus University. Bones Washington, a freshman, quickly captured her attention as an attentive student, sitting in the front row of her introductory biology class. Bones never missed class on Monday and Wednesday. But he was conspicuously absent every Friday. Johnson wondered why.

The day the first biology examination papers were returned, Washington waited till everyone else had left, then approached the professor. He was obviously self-conscious about a congenital jaw deformity. With his hand covering his jaw and his eyes turned down, talking to the floor, he said he could not understand why he had made only a score of 83 because he had studied "a whole bunch". He still hoped to achieve an "A" grade in the course.

In her usual caring way, professor Johnson suggested that one thing he might do was to attend class on Fridays. "Friday?!" Bones Washington said. He was stunned. And at that point, he opened up. He was the youngest of nine children, and his mother was ambivalent about his leaving home. She had intercepted his mail from Omnibus and destroyed his enrollment information. He became aware that classes had started that fall only when he read about it in the newspaper. He rushed to campus for late registration, but found most courses already full.

He and his faculty adviser worked hard until he was successfully enrolled in four courses. One was Biology 001. In completing his enrollment, a clerk carelessly stamped a seal on the lower right corner of his trial plan of study. That seal obliterated the "F" of the "MWF" which indicated the class meetings scheduled each week. This explained why conscientious Bones Washington attended only on Mondays and Wednesdays. He simply was too naive to know that most three-credit lecture courses meet three class hours weekly.

Bones's classroom participation and examination scores improved when he began attending Friday classes, and he earned the "A" he sought.

At the end of the semester, Bones asked professor Johnson what other courses he would need to complete before applying to medical school. For some reason, Bones had not been assigned to a pre-medicine adviser, and he had been enrolled in the introductory biology course intended for non-major students. So he might need to start all over by enrolling in the course for major and pre-professional students. Johnson arranged for Washington to be assigned to a pre-medicine adviser who could provide better academic counseling.

During the next seven semesters, Bones Washington kept in touch with professor Johnson, whose sincere interest in him continued. He was mentioned in the student newspaper from time to time for his high scholarship and noteworthy leadership on campus. Upon completing the baccalaureate degree, Washington was accepted by a ranked medical school for its next entering class. Today he is engaged in a busy family medicine practice in a working-class suburb of the capital city.

ℒ ℒ ℒ

Thanks to caring faculty members, Donald Franklin, Brenda Upcreek, and Bones Washington were able to navigate the treacherous shoals of the academy. Some students have not been so fortunate.

Kathy Kelly earned her place as class valedictorian over 300 students in a public high school in a midwestern state. As with many top students, Kathy began surveying places to pursue a college education during her sophomore year in high school. She narrowed her list to seven. Her parents encouraged Kathy, even though they could not afford to send her to college. She was determined to attend college, and made a firm resolve to become a social worker. But where would the money come from?

Kathy's aunt in another state encouraged her to enroll in Omnibus University – about an hour from the aunt's home – and offered to pay the out-of-state tuition. With her academic track record, Kathy was offered a large private scholarship at Omnibus, an institution that only a few years earlier was awarding nearly a half million dollars worth of tuition waivers to student-athletes, but less than $30,000 to all other undergraduates combined.

> Decide on what you think is right and stick to it.
> **George Eliot (1819-1880)**
> **English novelist**

The letter informing Kathy Kelly of her scholarship provided that, for so long as she maintained a 3.5 grade-point average (A=4.0), the support would be renewed. She accepted the scholarship, the challenge to achieve high grades, and earned straight-A grades her freshman year. So, with the scholarship, the financial assistance promised by her aunt, and the money she would earn in summer employment, the financing of Kathy's entire college education seemed assured. That was, until three weeks before classes were to resume in the fall.

While visiting her aunt one long weekend in late July, Kathy decided to visit Omnibus and confirm that all was well with enrollment and finances for her second year. In the Office of Financial Aid, she was shocked to learn that, because the university had over-committed its private scholarship funds, it would not be providing scholarships to any out-of-state students that year.

What would she do? Upon inquiring further, Kathy received a cold response: "Yes, it is final." To whom could she turn? Was the decision *absolutely* final?

From out of the blue, Kathy remembered meeting Dr. Maria Martinez, vice-president for student affairs, during a reception for honors students. In a split second, a committed and motivated Kathy Kelly decided to take her case to Dr. Martinez.

Kathy Kelly realized that a fast resolution would be needed if she were going to be able to attend Omnibus in a few weeks. So she retreated to the student center, bought a Coke (after the vending machine "ate" three quarters in a row), wrote a three-page letter, and hand-carried it to the vice-president's office. She explained the urgency of the matter to the receptionist.

Within minutes, an assistant vice-president learned that, due to a computer problem, students were late in being notified of the unfortunate shortfall that would mean no private scholarships that year for out-of-state students. She reconfirmed that, even though Kathy Kelly had been promised a year earlier that, provided she attained high grades, her scholarship would be renewed, now that commitment would not be honored.

Kathy was in shock. The assistant took her letter to the vice-president and explained the situation. The vice-president's eyes froze on Kathy's words, "I feel the university has not kept its promise to me. My 4.0 gpa is the highest possible." Dr. Martinez asked to see the student.

Kathy apologized for bringing her problem to the vice-president, but explained the importance of the terrible news she had received less than an hour earlier. After listening to Kathy's story and learning more about her background and interests, the vice-president asked if she had applied for part-time work. She replied that she had, but was told that in-state students would receive top priority, and that this year most of those funds were limited, too. Kathy added that she had extensive clerical experience.

The timing seemed too good to be true. Martinez had decided earlier that week that another part-time student assistant would be added to her support team. Kathy Kelly seemed exceptionally well-qualified. After a brief conference with her assistant, Martinez offered the part-time job to Kathy, who accepted the position right then and there. She worked in the vice-president's office until she graduated three years later.

Today, Kathy Kelly is a distinguished Omnibus alumna, having dedicated her life to social work with foster children in her hometown.

ℰ ℰ ℰ

Jade Johnson enrolled at Omnibus University to study mass communications. She achieved an average academic performance her first year, but encountered serious health problems the next year. By the time that summer rolled around, she found herself on academic probation.

Jade returned home for the summer only to run into the worst flood in the state's recorded history. Her family was forced to leave their home and live much of the summer in tents pitched in a series of relatives' back yards. Needless to say, worries about the flood and the living situation disrupted Jade's life all summer long.

In late August, Jade Johnson returned to campus shortly before the fall semester was to begin. She bought books required for the courses in which she had enrolled, moved into an apartment shared with two other students, and prepared to begin her junior year. A few days before the semester began, however, a letter delivered to her home address notified her that she had been placed on academic suspension for poor grades and her enrollment had been canceled.

Jade went immediately to the Office of Student Affairs, wanting to know the procedure to follow for appealing academic suspension. She believed her health problems explained her poor academic performance.

At that point, the ominous bureaucratic policies and rules of Omnibus University kicked in. The regulations stated that any student who was suspended had a limited period in which to appeal the action. For students suspended at the end of spring semester, this amounted to five business days after the semester closed. While this might have made good sense for students planning to enroll in summer school, it imposed a hardship on those who had already left campus and gone on to summer jobs or, as in Jade's case, encountered personal problems during the summer.

An assistant vice-president for student affairs decided Jade Johnson's case should be heard, and told her to gather the necessary documentation and to file an appeal. She did that. Not only did she provide documentation of her health problems, but her home town postmaster wrote a letter indicating that much of the mail there had been lost in the flood, and locating people whom the flood had displaced had delayed deliveries for weeks in some cases.

When the Academic Probation and Suspension Appeals Board met to hear cases of students suspended after summer session, they reviewed Jade Johnson's case. They perfunctorily decided not to rescind her suspension. Their reason: The rules did not permit them to hear her case once she had missed the spring appeals meeting, regardless of the circumstances.

Jade Johnson sat out two semesters before returning to Omnibus.

∽ ∽ ∽

Here it is not what the system can do for you, but rather what you can do to make the system work for you. You have to fight it.

Sophomore student at a large public university

"Fighting it" sometimes pays off. Randy Roberts, an Army veteran with nearly nine years of service, including two overseas assignments, was approved for early release from the military to enroll for the spring semester at Omnibus University. Arriving mid-year, he found few satisfactory alternatives on the apartment market, and was generally slow settling into the routines of college life. When several apartments became available at semester's end, Randy quickly upgraded his housing. He also took a summer job at a local computer repair shop.

It is common practice at most institutions of higher education, including Omnibus University, to mail letters at the end of each semester notifying students, who are being placed on academic probation or suspension, of their status. The letter includes a provision that, if extenuating circumstances seem to warrant reinstatement, an appeal may be made to the Academic Probation and Suspension Appeals Board. The appeals board meets only three times annually, soon after each academic session ends.

Serious problems invariably arise when students do not receive their letter of notice. Suspended students sometimes do not learn that their enrollment has been canceled until they return to campus to start the next semester of studies. By that time, they usually have signed a housing contract, arranged for part-time work, bought books for the courses in which they have pre-enrolled, among other commitments.

Such was the case for Randy Roberts. Upon learning his fate, he went directly to the office of the vice-president for student affairs, Maria Martinez. An office clerk told him that nothing could be done since he had failed to meet the deadline for filing an appeal.

By now Randy Roberts was rested and ready to address the rigors and routines of college life. He persisted in his request to discuss the matter with the vice-president. Randy told the vice-president that he had not received any notice of suspension. She told him the record indicated that the letter had been mailed, to such-and-such address. That address was obsolete, Randy said, and the letter apparently had not been forwarded.

The vice-president immediately moved to the next standard reply: As is clearly stated in the university catalog, it is the student's responsibility to notify the institution of any address change. Randy Roberts maintained that he had, in fact, notified the registrar's office of his new address. Martinez questioned this, since the address to which the suspension letter had been mailed was provided by the registrar. Further discussion revealed that Randy Roberts had indeed notified the financial aid office and his faculty adviser of the address change. He simply (but erroneously) assumed that, once one office on campus entered his new address into its computer, the change would be reflected in other offices across the campus.

The student told vice-president Martinez that during a lengthy stint in the military, the Pentagon had been able to keep accurate records of his duty locations all over the world. Further, he could not understand why Omnibus University – a quiet, one-location institution – could not communicate a simple address change among offices located in the same building!

Maria Martinez recognized the potential for institutional embarrassment and exercised good judgment when she granted Randy Roberts an administrative reinstatement.

$$\mathscr{L} \ \mathscr{L} \ \mathscr{L}$$

When budgetary dark clouds roll in, the superchargers of self-survival conduce. There is a tendency among administrators – especially those at third- and fourth-tier institutions – to search in desperation for a quick-fix for budgetary woes. Tuition money, particularly that paid by out-of-state students, is grabbed for as the proverbial lifesaver in a ruse that could hardly be more abusive of students.

It had been a good recruiting year for Omnibus University overall, and an especially good one for the College of Engineering. In recent years, that college had been criticized for its decreasing student enrollment. The dean had been told to either get enrollment up or resign. Higher enrollment meant more tuition dollars collected from students and more funds in the form of state appropriated matching money. It also meant more customers for local business owners, who praised Omnibus administrators when enrollments went up and criticized them when they turned down.

The collective hard-work efforts of faculty, staff, students, and alumni of the college were rewarded by a hefty enrollment jump, bringing presidential and board praise of the college's dean. Proportionately, the largest increase in enrollment was in the number of international students, resulting in more out-of-state tuition income, thereby easing the budgetary shortfall, at least in the short run.

One enabling factor in all this was the fact that transcripts of students from many other countries are difficult to evaluate. This gives admission officers ample opportunity to apply personal judgment. At the monthly student enrollment meetings, it was clear that these staffers had gotten the word to be liberal in evaluating such transcripts. "We desperately need more students," the president had said repeatedly.

Enrollment numbers drive virtually every curricular and extracurricular program in academe. Auxiliary enterprises – for example, retiring bonds that financed the construction of residence halls, the student union program and its many services, the university bookstore, intramural sports, athletic facilities, student recreational facilities, vending, and many others – all directly depend on student enrollment.

Student retention is as critical as student recruitment. Faculty advisers were counseled to be lenient in interpreting policies on course load and sequencing so as to help students "succeed" academically. Faculty members serve as watchdogs of academic quality, but when they are told that their salary increases are to be linked with enrollment increases, many succumb, and academic integrity suffers.

A high proportion of the unusually large number of new international students that year came from wealthy families of oil-exporting countries. This was pointed out to the faculty, emphasizing at the same time the need for student retention. The engineering faculty responded by easing academic rigor through less demanding course loads, even to the point of advising enrollment in courses that did not satisfy requirements for a degree.

This strategy for targeted retention of high-paying international students worked well for about four years. Student grades held, and families back home were happy. Local merchants praised the university for the increased enrollment of international students, who spent large amounts of money and stayed in town over weekends and holidays.

Beginning around year four, however, the realities of students not having met graduation requirements on schedule surfaced. Many students and parents were concerned, and some became angry. A few arrived on the campus with legal counsel, saying they were holding the university responsible for not providing proper student advisement. Two had papers drawn up to sue the university.

Meanwhile, to keep enrollment numbers up, collect more tuition and fee money, and remain eligible for more state-appropriated monies for higher education, university and state coordinating-board policies were eased or ignored. This permitted in-state and out-of-state domestic students to continue on academic probation well beyond the prescribed time limit. Many students had a cumulative grade point average below 1.0. Some had been enrolled six, seven, eight or even more years, with no realistic hope of ever graduating. Still, their tuition checks and patronage of auxiliary enterprises were important parts of the university's budget formula.

$$\mathscr{A} \quad \mathscr{A} \quad \mathscr{A}$$

Betsy Moore, a first-semester Omnibus freshman, learned from a new friend – a sophomore – about the possibility of testing out of Spanish 101, a required course for her major. Betsy had done especially well in Spanish coursework for three years in high school. Also, she had been an exchange student in Spain for six months, where she fluently conversed in Spanish with members of the three families with whom she lived.

8:40 a.m. Monday. Betsy entered the Foreign Languages Department office, and asked the secretary about the process to take the advanced-placement examination for Spanish 101. She was directed to go to the Registrar's Office.

9:00 a.m. Monday. The line at the Registrar's Office counter was not very long, but moving slowly. After 20 minutes, Betsy remembered her 9:30 class and moved to the front and asked the clerk how to take the Spanish 101 test. The clerk gave her a credit-by-examination form, and instructed her to complete and return the form to the arts and sciences college office. Betsy headed to her rhetoric class.

1:30 p.m. Monday. After lunch with a friend, Betsy Moore took the form – complete with name, birthdate, class, major, marital status, local and home addresses, parents' names and marital status, religious preference, nationality, Social Security number, and other information requested – to the college student services office. There she was told that the form had to be reviewed and approved, and that she should return Tuesday for the result.

3:40 p.m. Tuesday. Waiting her turn in line behind seven restless students, she watched the clerk dig her form from a 10-inch-high pile of unorganized papers, learned her request had been approved and that now she needed to take the form back to the Registrar's Office. Pressed to study with friends for an examination the following day, Betsy returned to her dorm room instead.

8:10 a.m. Wednesday. Bright and early, Betsy went to the Registrar's Office and presented her approved credit-by-examination form to the same clerk with whom she had dealt two days earlier. The woman advised Betsy that at that point the Registrar's Office had to determine whether her high school Spanish credits and grades were up to par, and that she should return Thursday.

9:40 a.m. Thursday. Betsy returned to the Registrar's Office, where the same clerk informed her that all requirements had been met and instructed Betsy to take the form to the Student Testing Service for assignment of a section number.

10:10 a.m. Thursday. A staffer at Student Testing assigned a section number, then directed Betsy back to the Registrar's Office for preliminary enrollment. In the process, she missed her 10:30 class.

1:30 p.m. Thursday. Betsy registered for Spanish 101 at the Registrar's Office, where her favorite clerk advised that now she had to return to her college student services office to schedule the examination.

1:50 p.m. Thursday. The clerk in the college office lifted a large calendar from atop a file cabinet and went over possible dates and times for the test. Betsy agreed on three weeks from Friday.

5:10 p.m. Friday. After three hours of part-time work in the Alumni Association office, Betsy called home to let her parents know she would not be home till around noon Saturday, because she had had a busy week, and she was tired and out of sorts.

ॐ ॐ ॐ

Ron Bath came from a family of modest means, and found attending college possible only through scholarships, 60-hours-a-week summer work, and three part-time jobs during the school year. One campus employment opportunity was weekend work in the university food service center.

While washing drinking glasses one Sunday morning, near the end of his shift, Ron sustained a deep cut on the palm of his left hand. Ron's supervisor told him to go immediately to the Student Health Center. He wrapped his hand in paper towels, stuck it in his pants pocket, and clocked out.

Ron Bath knew several staff members at the clinic from delivering food to the satellite cafeteria there. Upon arrival, he proceeded to the admissions station – holding folded, blood-soaked paper towels tightly over the cut. The receptionist gave him a two-page form to complete, then called Jessica Wampler, the nurse-in-charge that morning.

After filling out the form right-handed, southpaw Ron Bath gave it to the nurse, who requested more information before asking him why he had come. Ron removed the paper towels and showed her his injured hand.

The nurse thought several sutures would be required to close the wound. But rather than contacting the physician on call at that point, she first stuck a thermometer into Ron Bath's mouth. By that time Ron was becoming perturbed. "Why now?" he wanted to know. The nurse replied, "Our order is to get the temperature of every patient first – just standard procedure, you know." After more than another hour, a physician arrived, administered a local anesthetic, and made the seven stitches it took to close the cut and stop the bleeding.

> Well-entrenched institutions are usually the last to respond to change which occurs all about them.
> **Edward Danforth Eddy, Jr.**
> *Colleges for Our Land and Times:*
> *The Land-Grant Idea in American Education*
> **Harper & Brothers, New York, 1956**

> Action is eloquence.
> **William Shakespeare (1564-1616)**
> **English dramatist and poet**
> **from *Coriolanus***

REMEMBERING ... *The Tales of Two Students*

While speculation over the reasons for declining public support make for interesting conversation around the faculty lunch table, the more important task has been figuring out how to replace lost state revenue. The heaviest burden has fallen on students, who are paying much higher tuition, as well as a variety of extra "fees," are receiving fewer student services and in some cases are finding it difficult to get needed classes ... . To meet ... increased student demand under conditions of stable or relatively minor budgetary increases, higher education is obligated to reform significantly and to become more cost-effective.

The California Higher Education Policy Center
Crosstalk, **October 1994, pp. 4-6**

To pay for their education, graduates today are accruing staggeringly large student loans and entering the real world under a heavier burden of debt than their parents or older siblings racked up in decades of adult life. From 1990 to 1995 alone, college students borrowed more than $100 billion – as much as the total amount borrowed for education in the 1960s, '70s, and '80s combined.

Kathy Martin O'Neil, *Notre Dame Magazine*
Vol. 25, No. 4, Winter 1996-1997

Such totally uncontrollable expenditures, without any visible improvement in either the content or the quality of education, means that the system is rapidly becoming untenable. Higher education is in deep crisis.

Peter F. Drucker, Professor of Management
Peter F. Drucker Graduate Management Center of the Claremont
Graduate School, Interview published in *Forbes*, **March 10, 1997**

It is instructive and not a little frightening ... to compare the average four-year costs (tuition, fees, room and board) charged by both private and public baccalaureate institutions with median household incomes over the last two decades. The result is essentially a ratio that charts in constant dollars what people earn against what they are being asked to pay either for their own or their children's postsecondary education. As recently as 1975, median household income was nearly 30 percent more than the cost of four years at a private institution and three times more than the cost of four years at a public institution. By 1994 the cost of attending a private institution for four years was twice the median income of American households.

These ratios provide a ready explanation for the increased focus on costs that has come to dominate the public's scrutiny of American higher education. It is not just that cost increases have exceeded the rate of inflation. Rather, what occasions public anxiety is that sense of being asked to pay more for less in terms of likely earnings in relation to stated prices.

Policy Perspectives, **May 1997, Vol. 7 No. 2**
(Supported by John S. & James L. Knight Foundation & The Pew Charitable Trusts)

CHAPTER 10

COMBATING DRY ROT
IN THE IVORY TOWER:
FUMIGATION, VENTILATION, AND
RENEWAL OF THE ACADEMIC
SANCTUARY

When we think of education as an investment, it be-
comes something not to be economized but emphasized.
Nowhere is there an illiterate peasantry that is progressive.
Nowhere is there a literate peasantry that is not.

John Kenneth Gailbraith (b. 1908)
Canadian-American economist

All that is necessary for evil to triumph is for good men
to do nothing.

Edmund Burke (1729-1797)
British statesman and orator

It is the responsibility of an author who has laid out its
signs to offer suggestions for reducing *dry rot in the ivory tower.*
Fortunately, others will have different ideas and approaches to
effect remedies. A diverse, generalized ferment is just what is

needed to generate the widespread, fervent determination to fumigate, ventilate, and renew the academic sanctuary, which is so clearly indicated.

> Don't find fault. Find a remedy.
> What's right about America is that, although we have a mess of problems, we have great capacity – intellect and resources – to do something about them.
> **Henry Ford (1863-1947)**
> **American automobile manufacturing pioneer**

Whatever problems exist in academe today, our nation has sufficient human resources, ideas, and wherewithal to success-fully deal with them. Of course, blazing one's way across contentious territory is never easy. But the leaders of higher education must start and stay the course – remain accountable to the public trust; mediate the often conflicting perspectives of faculty members and administrators; preserve and bolster the spirits of creative inquiry and mentoring that are the essence of scholarship and pedagogy.

The history of every great institution of higher education began in the hearts of men and women who were inspired by altruism, optimism, and vision. The kind who strove to improve outcomes for students and society in the first place will also be the rebuilders of institutional excellence. But before any such renewal can happen, regardless of how necessary and regardless of the determination of the rebuilders, effective fumigation followed by thorough ventilation are needed to wipe out the *dry rot* in the academic sanctuary that is *the ivory tower*.

> Determine that the thing can and shall be done ... and then we shall find the way.
> **Abraham Lincoln (1809-1865)**
> **Sixteenth President, United States of America**

I remain optimistic!

If I were omnipotent, my approach to making the higher academy well again would employ first the fundamental agencies of *forthright changes* effected by *courageous leaders*, supported by an *enlightened faculty*, and embraced by a *committed governing board*. This book is not the place to expound on an exhaustive list of remedial ways and means. The necessary medicines and surgeries are specific to each institution anyway. But the fundamentals I shall advance here hold across all academe.

> We should also talk about education as a way of conveying America's moral and political principles and nurturing the character of the young. We should speak about education in the context of human excellence, high standards and national greatness. We must demonstrate an understanding of, and a willingness to articulate and defend, the fundamental purpose of education, which is to engage in the architecture of the soul.
>
> **William J. Bennett (b. 1943)**
> **United States Secretary of Education (1985-1988)**
> **Current Co-Director, Empower America**
> **Fellow, Heritage Foundation**

⬮ ⬮ ⬮

Humans tend to want to do things in familiar ways so as to maintain balance, control, and security in their lives. Most changes engender anxiety and fear in most stakeholders.[1]

> Trying to bring about change and reform in the old bureaucracy is a little like trying to install an internal-combustion engine in a horse.
>
> **Don McCorkell, Jr. (b. 1947)**
> **Oklahoma legislator (1979-1995)**

> Faced with the choice between changing one's mind and proving that there is no need to do so, almost everyone gets busy on the proof.
>
> **John Kenneth Gailbraith (b. 1908)**
> **Canadian-American economist**

Because change has no constituency, educational institutions must intentionally develop ways and means of protecting and supporting those both wise enough to see the need for change and brave enough to tackle the job. As a start, *the ivory tower* should figuratively be set on fire, so everyone can see the flames, smell the smoke, sense the portents of doom, all without burning the place down. The denial of the need for revolutionary change up and down the line in *the ivory tower* is appalling.

> My most depressing finding was the degree to which ordinary people are perfectly happy to believe nonsense, as long as it makes them feel good.
> **Raphael S. Ezekiel (b. 1931)**
> **American author**

$$\mathscr{A} \; \mathscr{A} \; \mathscr{A}$$

$\mathscr{A}$ American universities have been able to virtually ignore public concerns about rising costs due to falling productivity up to now, primarily because a college education has sold so well on the job market. But that payoff is plateauing at the same time the cost of attaining a college degree is skyrocketing out of control, government funding is decreasing, and proportionately fewer traditional students are pursuing a college education.

> If you take some of the basic problems facing our society ... and then make a list of all the things that a university could contribute ... and ask yourself how do all these things rank in the list of priorities of the modern university, one is struck by how low they rank.
> **Derek Bok (b. 1930)**
> **President, Harvard University (1971-1991)**

> To improve is to change. To achieve perfection is to change often.
> **Sir Winston Churchill (1874-1965)**
> **Prime Minister, United Kingdom**
> **(1940-1945; 1951-1955)**

> Resistance to fundamental reform has been ingrained in the American collegiate and university tradition, and except on rare occasions, the historic policy of universities has been

one of drift, reluctant accommodation, belated recognition that while no one was looking, change had, in fact, taken place.

Frederick Rudolph (b. 1920)

♋ For one thing, higher education should be doing more with less, just as business firms recently have had to do in an increasingly competitive economy. Institutional policies, procedures, systems, and traditions – and the copious forms and other "hoops" apparently considered necessary to maintain them – provide the foundations and bricks for administrative walls; the complicated, excessive personnel policies, the mortar and reinforcing rods. An impudent, irresponsible, not-in-my-job-description! mentality – antithetical to innovation and ultimately dehumanizing – has been fostered, intentionally or not. Alas, a potent brew of make-no-waves administrators, tenured faculty, unionized nonteaching staff, protest-prone students, nostalgic alumni, reverent traditionalists, remote and athletics-oriented governing boards, and consensus-driven decision-making have effectively thwarted most efforts to downsize.

Colleges and universities should, nonetheless, examine each and every opportunity for putting the brakes on rising costs. The germane questions regarding each and every activity and service of the institution are: Does it support the institutional mission? If it *is* needed, would outsourcing or privatizing be less costly? If we *do* continue to provide it internally, how can we improve its efficiency?

> We must melt the fat out of the education bureaucracy: American business has restructured in the past 10 years and has proven that a lot of jobs were unnecessary. The Army is doing it. The Navy is doing it. The government is doing it. Education is not doing it.
>
> **Albert Gamper, Jr.**
> *The Wall Street Journal*, March 14, 1997, p. R-6

♋ Every opportunity to develop new sources of revenue also should be evaluated, and, if viable, vigorously initiated. As such entrepreneurial pursuits take root, however, institutional leaders often find they have opened themselves to criticism from local business people, who claim unfair competition due to the institution's tax-exempt status. Most university administrators are not business people, and tend to quickly pull their punches when brickbats start coming their way. Of course, political realities must be addressed by all parties, and statesmanship must be of the highest order. But universities simply must become more businesslike and more doggedly entrepreneurial.

> The university needs a considerable degree of autonomy and flexibility so that it has the freedom to teach and research without politicized interference, so that creativity and imagination are encouraged, and so resources (including the time and energy of faculty, staff, and students) are used efficiently. The university also needs the involvement of the state as a force for meeting the public's needs, as a force for change and as a force for accountability. The problem, therefore, is not to eliminate the state's role, but to perfect it.
>
> **Frank C. Newman (b. 1917)**
> **American legal educator**

𝒮 𝒮 𝒮

The academy's hickeys should be aggressively addressed if higher education expects to regain the public trust it needs in order to proceed with responsive programs. *Dry rot in the ivory tower* basically derives from accumulated errors in judgment, which in turn mostly flow from flawed moral compasses, from ethical codes gone awry. The pervasive unwillingness of administrators to assume responsibility for their decisions; their skilled, self-serving obfuscation and prevarication when confronted by uncomfortable or illegal situations (as daily they are); and their unscrupulous dependence on situational ethics – the childish notion that "anything goes", that a deserving end justifies any means – gave root in the first place to most of higher education's troubles today. *Dry rot in the ivory tower* has directly and indirectly resulted largely from lackadaisical, self-protective leaders. As Confucius observed, "Fish rot from the head down."

> What is right is not derived from the rule. The rule arises from our knowledge of what is right.
>> **Julius Paulus (2nd-3rd century AD)**
>> **Roman jurist**

> Situational ethics and moral relativism have replaced the bedrock American values.
>> **Kent C. Nelson**
>> **Chairman and CEO, United Parcel Service (1989-1996)**

✍ The damaged image of universities calls for courageous, energetic, indefatigable leaders having strong senses of vision and urgency, to kill and drive out the dry rot, replace it with more rational and responsive structures and more highly motivated and principled people, and then turn sour public attitudes about higher education sweet again. The hiring of top-notch administrators will be critical. Academe's leadership ranks need to be rejuvenated by men and women willing to exercise prudent judgment and then to take calculated risks on behalf of institutional interests.

> Take calculated risks. That is quite different from being rash.
>> **George Smith Patton (1885-1945)**
>> **General, United States Army**

> When you make changes, you do not make friends.
>> **Leo Kornfeld (b. 1932)**
>> **Former Vice-President, Pace University, New York**
>> **Special Assistant to U. S. Secretary of Education**
>> **for Student Loans**

> The problem with most of us is we would rather be ruined by praise than saved by criticism.
>> **Norman Vincent Peale (1898-1993)**
>> **American minister and author**

> We can't wait for the storm to blow over. We have to learn to work in the rain.
>
> **Cecil J. (Pete) Silas (b. 1932)**
> **Chairman and CEO, Phillips Petroleum Company**
> **(1985-1994)**

✍ True leadership begins by managing and minimizing the bureaucracy. Too often the administrative system is constipated by officialism – a lack of initiative, an inflexible adherence to rules, a penchant for policy proliferation. Rather than rock the boat, and thereby risk criticism, most people working in such an environment eventually give in and give up, and become content to muddle through a set of mundane, often superfluous tasks day after day.

> One way to avoid criticism is to do nothing. Then the world will not bother you.
>
> **Napoleon Bonaparte (1769-1821)**
> **Emperor of France (1804-1815)**

> There has always been room for innovation and fresh starts in American higher education, even if this freedom, which rested partly on expanding enrollments and funds, is more circumscribed now. What is really lacking is strong and visionary academic leadership.
>
> **David Riesman (b. 1909)**
> **American social scientist**

✍ An effective vision statement combines gut values with concrete objectives. It will have a tangible outcome and project an inspiring image of an improved future, something achievable but almost out of reach. *Status-quo* members of the faculty often will criticize a progressive leader for being a dreamer, a Pollyannish utopian who ignores the details of current problems, but then they will tend to go on to claim that he has no vision! In fact, his vision may have been clearly defined. The faculty and staff simply did not agree with it (nor would they have agreed with *any* vision requiring substantive change).

When a progressive administrator beseeches faculty members to change, he often soon finds himself looking down a rifle barrel, which triggers self-protective instincts. Consequently, many of today's academic leaders will not even proffer a vision. They choose instead to respond to events rather than intentionally prepare for them or try to influence their course.

> Self-serving spinelessness, not ideology, is what has led to the current catastrophe in our universities.
>
> From *The Shadow University:*
> *The Betrayal of Liberty on America's Campuses*
> by **Alan C. Kors** and **Harvey A. Silverglate**
> Copyright © 1998 by Harvey A. Silverglate and Alan C. Kors
> Reprinted with permission of The Free Press,
> a Division of Simon & Schuster, Inc.

🔊 Nowadays, sadly, when an outstanding faculty member is encouraged to assume an administrative position in the academy, he or she commonly faces a dilemma: a choice between the potential excitement of demonstrating leadership, on the one hand, and hesitancy to subject one's self and family to the demands and drawbacks of such a role, on the other. As official harbingers of bad news and endless woes, university line administrators at all levels serve as close-range targets for discontented faculties.

> The visionary leader has to establish himself as a spokesman for the interests of society in performing, in achieving ... . He has to become the proponent, the educator, the advocate ... .
>
> **Peter F. Drucker (b. 1909)**
> **Austro-American futurist**

🔊 You cannot improve something if you cannot control it; you cannot control it if you cannot understand it; you cannot understand it if you cannot measure it. Three forces external to the university – accreditation and regulatory pressures, the growth of consumerism, and the quality-management movement – make program assessment a compelling agenda item for higher education today. Institutional reports should inform the public with a comprehensive overview of the organization and how data are used in decision-making processes.

Outputs measure the service provided, *outcomes* the results of those outputs. The number of students graduating is a parameter of *output*, whereas *outcome* measures include such things as employer satisfaction with graduates' performance as employees and the success of graduates in gaining admission to postgraduate schools. *Accountability* amounts to an administrator's being responsible for producing acceptable *outcomes*. Administrators must be willing to be *accountable* – to taxpayers, students, and employers of graduates, among others.

ℒ ℒ ℒ

> Few governing boards have the competence or the inclination to be innovative, to be experimental, to chart new courses. By their very nature governing boards tend to conserve what is and seek new paths only when a crisis is clearly at hand.
>
> **John D. Millet (b. 1912)**
> **President, Miami University of Ohio (1953-1964)**

ℒ   Vision and follow-through should go hand in hand. Governing boards and administrators should make and then stand by the necessary, tough decisions that have resulted from due process. Leaders do right things; managers do things right. Administrators today must be part leader and part manager (and that is a tall order). The responsible leader should first proffer a vision. Governing boards – with a light touch of oversight as their public mandate – should exercise their collective responsibility to fine-tune and confirm that vision, and then empower the responsible manager to do things right in the follow-through.

> State boards result in unnecessary layers of bureaucracy. In terms of time, money, and initiatives, the cost is heavy .... . Many boards have begun to function as miniature governments ...
>
> **James L. Fisher**
> **President, Towson State University (1968-1978)**
> **"The Failure of Statewide Coordination,"**
> *The Chronicle of Higher Education*, **June 16, 1995, p. A48**

✍ In general, more attention should be given to the search for and selection of governing board members. When people seek a seat on a university governing board for the wrong reasons, board effectiveness suffers. Too often, appointment or nomination decisions are based on power cliques or money contributed to foundations or political campaigns rather than on a record of interest, competence, or strong leadership and service in the important, complex matters of higher education.

✍ For public institutions, the search and selection process for governing board members should involve interested individuals submitting their credentials to a special committee comprised primarily of institutional alumni and supporters. This committee should screen applications and (depending on the system) either present the names of candidates considered qualified to those responsible for the appointment or, serving as a nominating committee, present the slate to those who will vote.

> If I were to suggest what I consider to be most important for the future of the university, I should put priority on a system that would assure that the board of trustees be constituted of men and women with a real interest in education ... .
>
> **John A. Hannah (1902-1991)**
> **President, Michigan State University (1941-1969)**

✍ A typical case in point is the board's role in the governance of intercollegiate athletics. Athletics are rooted in competition, which brings out both the best and the worst in people, leading to both favorable and unfavorable headlines.

The taxpaying public generally expects three things of intercollegiate athletics programs. First, the university's academic standards should be the same for athletes as for nonathletes. An individual who reports to the institution's chief academic officer should provide oversight for athletes' academic matters, including class attendance, tutoring, and progress toward degree attainment. Second, strict compliance with all policies, rules, and laws is the responsibility of every person associated in any way with intercollegiate athletics. An independent compliance officer should oversee all germane matters and report directly to the president, the official ultimately responsible for compliance. Third, the institution should have a rational strategic plan for financing intercollegiate athletics and a stringent structure of financial oversight. Governing board members meddle in the athletics program more than anything else. Board interference of any kind with the athletics program must not be tolerated.

ॐ ॐ ॐ

Higher education would do well to shift attention away from perfunctory five-year plans and organizational charts and toward people and processes, from which excellence in teaching, research, and public service derives. It should strive to eliminate factors that hamper motivated people, and it should encourage and reward collaboration, promote access to information, and measure and reward achievement of defined objectives.

ॐ The authority of today's administrators at most universities – the ability to make much-needed change and progress – is gravely compromised by the general expectation that faculty consensus enjoys absolute veto power over policy initiatives. This situation is fatuous. For one thing, faculty members almost always hold disparate views on what the character of the institution ought to be, so consensus-driven systems are doomed to honor *status quo*. Although this trend has not been useful, it has nonetheless been pervasive and robust.

> Perhaps the largest problem is that piece of academic culture that requires collegial consensus and the leadership of leading faculty and institutions before the bulk of academe will consent to break new ground. Clearly this greatly slows the process of innovation and improvement.
>
> **Jerrier Haddad**

⚗ The folkways that reinforce ingrained practices in the academic ivory tower are tenaciously held and zealously protected. They are so pervasive and powerful, in fact, that it is almost impossible for most faculty members to imagine, let alone accept, real change. Most faculty members can be creative and innovative. This comes mostly within frameworks set by discipline-based habits and rules, however; it is generally not determined by emergent societal imperatives and opportunities.

> A great civilization is not conquered from without until it has destroyed itself within.
>
> **William J. Durant (1885-1981)**
> *Caesar and Christ* **(1944)**

⚗ The media thrive on conflict, especially conflict among parties having any stake in an enterprise as important as higher education. Programs should be designed to bring faculty members in effective touch with the public and its representatives. Faculty members should regularly meet with local education leaders, elected public officials and servants, business people, alumni, and the media, to discuss concerns and issues. Otherwise, they will be unable to be responsive.

⚗ Faculty members' chronic complaints about underfunding coincide with compelling charges that higher education of late has not been responding to public needs. Higher education faculties should expect to be supported financially only to the extent they provide the services the public needs and wants. The faculty must recognize that no administrator can re-order such things.

> Hard times are producing nothing less than a complete change in the character of our institutions of higher learning. Every aspect of their work is being affected. Their faculty, their students, their organizations, their methods, their teaching, and their research are experiencing such alteration

that we who knew them in the good old days shall shortly be unable to recognize them. Many of these changes are for the better. Others may wreck the whole system.

Robert Maynard Hutchins (1899-1977)
President, University of Chicago (1929-1951)

As society came to rely more and more on the universities, universities in turn grew ever more dependent on society for the money required to support their expanding activity.

Derek Bok (b. 1930)
President, Harvard University (1971-1991)

The higher education community thinks they're above it all. They don't like to be told what to do. But if they want us to be their sugar daddy, there are going to be some rules.

Wayne M. Jones (b. 1954)
Ohio legislator (1988-1996)

⅗ Faculties must come to face all sorts of facts. In the past, stability in institutions of higher education was the norm, change the anomaly. In the future, it will be the other way around. One way or another, the roles of the faculty in the academy are going to be restructured. It will be a monumental undertaking. That figurative fire in the ivory tower will help provoke people to act on this reality.

Better to take change by the hand before it takes you by the throat.

Sir Winston Churchill (1874-1965)
Prime Minister, United Kingdom
(1940-1945; 1951-1955)

We must recognize that reform will not be easy, that the system fails because it is set up to fail, and that the professoriate – a profession run amok and without responsibility or accountability to students, society, or learning – will guard its prerogatives ferociously.

Charles J. Sykes (b. 1954)
***ProfScam* (1988), p. 257**

✄ And then there is the long-standing albatross of academic tenure. Faculty members have traditionally decided which fledgling colleagues would have a permanent place to work in the academy. This outmoded system raises a deep-orange warning flag for a taxpaying public that is already suspicious about the motives and processes of the people running higher education today. Defenders of the academic tenure system should know that arguments about academic freedom and the like ring hollow to those outside the academy, whose growing employment instability in these times of business downsizing makes the arrangement seem to be a luxurious entitlement.

For the tenure system to survive, the threat of its denial should not be used to stifle free speech. Academic freedom should be used only for its originally intended purpose, namely, to protect scholarship *per se* from political interference. And academic tenure should be granted much more sparingly. It would make more sense to have a system wherein many faculty members are hired on a year-to-year basis – for perhaps 30 years in a row – but never tenured. Interestingly, the same professors who are disdainful of the union work rules for certain nonteaching staff members, without thinking, take the rightness of tenure for granted.

> The educator ... may turn his podium into an ideological pulpit and then get all huffy at the mere suggestion that he's strayed from his responsibilities. Before tenure, he is accountable only to his like-minded peers. After tenure, he's accountable to no one, least of all the public or university supporters paying his salary.
>
> **Richard K. Armey (b. 1940)**
> **Former university professor**
> **Member, U. S. House of Representatives**
> **(1985-present)**

Tenure has become a legislative target and exaggerates the disconnection of faculty from the broader community. The professoriate has not effectively articulated the social meaning of tenure – the protection of the university as a

place where inconvenient questions can be asked, and not a
job protection for a specially sheltered status group.
R. Eugene Rice
New Pathways 32
Working Paper Series Inquiry #1 (1996), p. 32
American Association for Higher Education, Washington, DC

There is one more negative point regarding the tenure system. Higher education serves as a major custodian of our
nation's cultural heritage. Although society needs certain shared
traditions and values to achieve stability, paradoxically, diversity
also engenders strength. Higher education provides an excellent
forum for these essential diverse views. In practice, the
academic tenure system greatly hampers an institution's
attempts to change by diversifying.

$\mathscr{D}$ $\mathscr{D}$ $\mathscr{D}$

Education has in America's whole history been the
major hope for improving the individual and society.
Gunnar Myrdal (1898-1987)
Swedish economist

---

[1] "The Dynamics of Change," Chapter 11 (pp. 185-200), *Reclaiming A
Lost Heritage: Land-Grant and Other Higher Education Initiatives for
the Twenty-First Century*, Campbell, John R., Michigan State University Press, East Lansing, MI, 1998

REMEMBERING ... *The Tales of Two Students*

College costs are out-of-control: they have grown nearly three times as fast as inflation and twice as fast as the general economy ... . Although today's colleges and universities look much like large business corporations with thousands of employees (i.e., faculty and staff) and millions of customers (i.e., students and parents), they are not organized or run like a business ... . What we are seeing today is an S&L style financial crisis: Although higher education appears thriving and prosperous on the surface, vast instability and corruption lie just below. The question is, "How long can the veneer last?" What finally broke the savings and loan institutions was a combination of bureaucratic meddling, a credit crunch after years of "easy money," and the industry's own chronic mismanagement and massive overinvestment. That combination is precisely what threatens colleges and universities today ... . More money did not bail out the failing S&Ls in the 1980s; they simply misspent it in the same ways they had been misspending for years. Failing businesses only recover when they engage in a fundamental restructuring of the way they do business.

George Roche, President, Hillsdale College
Imprimis, **October 1994, pp. 3,5,6**
(Monthly journal of Hillsdale College, reprinted by permission)

Public schools too often fail because they are shielded from the very force that improves performance and sparks innovation in nearly every other human enterprise – competition. In business, in the professions, even in our private lives, we rarely muster the courage to improve performance without external challenge.

Robert Lutz and Clark Durant
The Wall Street Journal, **September 20, 1996, p. A14**

Even as education opens up worlds of opportunity, education debt can narrow those opportunities to the jobs that can pay the bills. Some graduates with heavy debt burdens can't afford to take lower-paying public service jobs – as rural teachers, public defenders, community health providers – and still make their loan payments.

Kathy Martin O'Neil
Notre Dame Magazine, **Vol. 25, No. 4, Winter 1996-1997**

Universities have an exalted mission, but as they become rich and bloated, they appear more arrogant and greedy – a special-interest group more interested in dollars than truth and beauty.

Richard Vedder, Economics Professor, Ohio University
"Higher Education at a Lower Cost"
Wall Street Journal, **August 31, 1998, p. A18**

Epilogue

A good beginning makes a good ending.

English Proverb

High above the tallest trees, in the shadow of the mountains, where sunlight turns to glistening gold and the spirit of freedom resides, only there can you expect to find the majestic bald eagle, the unchallenged ruler of the skies, the mighty symbol of strength, endurance, and freedom. With its powerful wings spread in glorious display, the eagle soars with grandeur into the sun, circling confidently over its domain of rugged mountains, elegant trees, and lush valleys. The eagle's call speaks of courage, confidence, and power. Little wonder it has become an enduring symbol of those things we embrace and hold dear, of the American dream.

The American dream – the inborn ambition that inspires and drives each man and woman to actualize his or her potential – has come to reality through our educational institutions, our democratic form of government, and our free-enterprise system. Imbued with firm convictions that higher education's role in the American dream needs people to play the part of Hans at the dike, to spread the inhibitors of *dry rot*, to transform *the ivory tower*, I have tried to communicate a message not with ambiguity but with clarity, not with reservation but with candor. Knowing my views will be questioned and criticized, I nevertheless wanted to join the debate that is so very critical at this time.

This book comprises a compendium of anecdotes and words of others I believe will be useful in re-calibrating academe's moral compass. It embodies accepted, time-honored understandings of the values and virtues important inside as well as outside *the ivory tower.* These lessons and reminders can help in rejuvenating the once-but-no-longer highly favorable relationship of trust between the public and its higher education academy.

Many of the ideas and philosophies shared here speak, with neither hesitation nor embarrassment, to the inner core of human individuals, to their personal morals and values, the basic ethics by which we live.

> Morality for each one of us is our own conscience, not what is popular or easy.
>
> **Theodore M. Hesburgh (b. 1917)**
> **President, University of Notre Dame (1952-1987)**

Dry rot in the ivory tower is not a plague that came on suddenly. Rather it has been a contagious, insidious, relentless, chronic disease. And time to effect a remedy is running out. Members of the higher education family should adopt a philosophy along the lines of: "This is my institution, right or wrong; when right to be kept right, when wrong to be put right." Measures must be taken to inhibit *dry rot in the ivory tower.* Members of the academy must come to grips with tough decisions and move ahead in resolving the most pressing matters, lest higher education experience even further deterioration of public trust and support.

Higher education has a rich heritage to preserve and extend. Each generation since the Pilgrims has known its particular problems and privations. But each has found the courage and determination to overcome adversity. Throughout the more than two hundred years since gaining our independence, the people of this great nation have found ways to overcome obstacles of all kinds and to succeed against odds of all sorts. Our best and most enduring qualities – charity, compassion, ingenuity, integrity, moral commitment, optimism, and resilience – have had ways of resurfacing when we needed them most.

I know who holds the future. I have a deep and abiding faith in the future of those who make up the core of the academic family. They comprise a dedicated group of people of all walks who I believe will accept the clear challenges at hand, jump eagerly to meet new crises and fulfill new opportunities, and once again demonstrate that there is extraordinary potential in ordinary people.

So let us go forth from here and now, confident in our lofty aspirations; strong and unwavering in our commitment to education; inspired by a vision of an even greater system of higher education in the twenty-first century; sustained by faith in students and our other clienteles; and motivated by an intense desire to better serve the public, of which we are an integral part.

> But the bravest are surely those who have the clearest vision of what is before them, glory and danger alike, and yet, notwithstanding, go out to meet it.
> **Thucydides (ca. 400 BC)**
> **Greek historian**

INDEX

173